KU-353-794

In the manner of the famous Henry Root series of spoof letters of the 1970s, humorist Andy Bain has hooked in Scottish politicians with his individual line in public participation.

Posing as a dotty retired doctor with nothing better to do than make comment on personal appearance, a Rangers-supporting Asian postmaster, an abusive pensioner busybody, or a right wing 'hang-'em-an-flog-'em' Green, the correspondence is hilarious. And makes telling comment on the state of our body politic.

Who said politics is boring? With Andy Bain, it's a case of Don't Vote for an idiot, Vote for a clown!

'I laughed till I nearly wet myself!'
Sunday Times Scotland

'The McRoot letters. . . gullibility
and vanity has been exposed.'
The Scotsman

'a 21st century epistolary exchange
with Scotland's political elite'
Big Issue

'howlers@holyrood'
Sunday Times

'gasbags@holyrood'
Daily Record

'Hoax was easy PC'
Daily Mail

Don't Vote
for an Idiot
Vote
for a Clown

Andy Bain

Argyll
publishing

© Andy Bain 2003
Argyll Publishing
Glendaruel
Argyll PA22 3AE

The author has asserted his
moral rights.

**British Library Cataloguing-
in-Publication Data.
A catalogue record for this
book is available from the
British Library.**

ISBN 1 902831 58 6

Cover drawings
Andy Bain

Typeset & Origination
Cordfall Ltd, Glasgow

Printing
Bell & Bain Ltd, Glasgow

For Helen and Amelia

Preface

On the 23rd of March 1979 Henry Root addressed the first of his many letters to Mrs Thatcher. The brilliant William Donaldson, the journalist behind The Henry Root Letters, sensed that Britain was on the precipice of a new era. Henry Root corresponded with politicians, Chief Constables, Captains of Industry, Fleet Street Editors and media personalities. His letters probed their hypocrisies, strange gullibilities and peculiar vanities.

With the arrival of 129 new Members in the first Scottish Parliament in 300 years it occurred to me that the same method could reveal some invaluable insights into our new Scottish democracy. There were far fewer landowners among the membership than the last time a parliament sat in Edinburgh – even to vote in those days you had to be a substantial property owner. But in the modern version, in order to get a sniff of government you simply have to be a party member and a loyal one.

I launched my campaign in May 2001 under the pseudonym of Archie Beatty. My first letter informed Lord Steel that I was in contact with extraterrestials. Instead of urging me to seek psychological help Sir David's secretary treated the correspondence as if it was perfectly normal!

For a month the response from the parliamentarians absolutely flooded in. Had they nothing better to do with their time? Then, the week Lord Archer was jailed for perjury, the replies suddenly ground to a shuddering halt. Jeffrey Archer was imprisoned because an incriminating diary he had ordered his secretary to destroy, thirteen years before, turned up intact. His secretary had destroyed the incriminating document but she had made a copy!!!

During the early days of the new Scottish Parliament there was also a problem with a diary. The Lobbygate Scandal, revealed that an employee of Beattie Media, Alex Barr, secretly filmed by the Observer newspaper, claimed he could put appointments directly into then Finance Minister Jack McConnell's constituency diary and that he had already done so. When the Parliament's Standards Committee asked to see the diary it was reported that this offending dairy also had been destroyed.

Archie Beatty had written claiming that Jack McConnell's secretary, just like Jeffrey Archer's, had failed to destroy the offending document and that a copy had come in to Archie's possession and that a prominent tabloid journalist was hectoring him to buy the diary. 'Jack, what should I do?'

I was perplexed. I had been getting replies from supposedly busy parliamentarians two and three times a day – then, nothing. Then I got a call from the tabloid journalist I had pretended was after the diary. He was after the diary!!! I explained to him that I was attempting to repeat the Henry Root scam. He couldn't tell me how he had obtained the e-mail but reported that there had been a violent loosening of the bowels on its receipt at the parliament (though, he used a shorter and couthier Scottish expression).

So my cover was blown and I became Dr Rosemary Hannay, a bluff Scottish 'dame d'un certain age'. About this time I was visited, at home, by two ugly members of the 'Parliamentary Police Unit'. The PPU is a security outfit that protects Scottish politicians from the electorate. They claimed they wanted to talk to me about a letter to Jim Wallace in which Archie had threatened to 'boot' a journalist up the backside on behalf of the Justice Minister. But they knew about all of my letters and appeared to be convinced that I had tried to blackmail Jack McConnell.

So I allowed the Sunday Times (Scotland) to do a front page feature on the letters in their 'Ecosse' section and I changed my nom de plume to Asinder Khan, sub-post master and staunch Rangers supporter.

After an exchange of opinions with Donald Gorrie MSP on sectarianism, Asinder was charged with 'wasting Police time' and a damaging full page report appeared in the Daily Record and Rupert Clubbs was born.

Rupert thrived for a while then suddenly all his correspondence dried up again. The last character to appear was Roberta Caldwell-Smyth a worried mother, church elder and representative of 'middle' Scotland.

The title needs some explanation. In the mid-1980s the immensely popular French comedian 'Coluche' stood for the French Presidency. His slogan was 'Don't vote for an Idiot, Vote for a Clown'. His campaign had the political elite rattled and he was approaching 20% in the polls. He withdrew from the race when his election agent was found dead, in mysterious circumstances, in a lay-by in northern France. At their last general election the French people had to choose between Le Pen, a fascist and Chirac, who most French people know is a crook. An idiot or a clown.

But, surely in Scotland it's not like that. We have plenty of choice? I hope, dear reader, you will be enlightened and entertained by a perusal of the correspondence with our leading politicians at the time of our new Scottish Parliament. The average Scottish political party animal an idiot or a clown? You can decide for yourself.

Andy Bain
February 2003

From: Rosemary Hannay [mailto:hannayrosemary@hotmail.com
Sent: 10 September 2001 11:02
To: wendy.alexander.msp@scottish.parliament.uk
Subject: Sunday Mail

Hello Wendy,

I am sure you are as scandalised as I am at the effrontery of Lindsay McGarvie and the Sunday Mail publishing a picture of you showing intimate items of your underwear. I went out with Lindsay at university and he was always a scum-sucking, bottom feeder!!

How would he like it if photos of him in his saggy elastic, grey underpants were exposed to his colleagues and contemporaries for their amusement and delectation? Well we can find out!! I have pictures of Lindsay posing in a pair of the aforementioned sad grey articles, his wee pot belly hanging over and his stupid face screwed up because he has lost his specs.

Of course the sub-text of publishing your photo was to ridicule and diminish a successful woman politician in advance of the reshuffle. The 4 small pictures at the side of the photo reveal his nefarious intentions. The first makes you look like an Iranian fanatic and the second and fourth show you in ludicrously abnormal poses. The third, where you are wearing a bizarre medical contraption on your head and laughing like a lunatic is intended to convey the impression that you are some dopey nutcase. (Unfortunately, it works.)

I will be in Edinburgh on Friday 15 Sept. professionally and will come into your office with the photos. (Can your staff be trusted as some of them are a bit saucy?) So unless I hear from you that it is inconvenient I'll pop through your door about 09:30 next Friday.

Dr. Rosemary Hannay

PS. Susan and Jackie should think about makeovers too (and diet sheets) and someone should buy Sarah a comb!

From: Anne-Marie Cooper@scottish.parliament.uk
To: Rosemary Hannay
Subject: Sunday Mail
Sent: 12 Sep 2001

Dr Hannay

Thank you for your email to Ms Alexander. I am sure she will very much appreciate your comments when she has a chance to catch up on her parliamentary emails.

Unfortunately, Ms Alexander will not be in Edinburgh on Friday and all her staff will be through at her ministerial office in Glasgow.

Your kind offer to let Ms Alexander view the photographs you have is very much appreciated but hope you will understand that Ms Alexander unfortunately will not have the time to spend with you. Thank you once again for your email and kind offer – it certainly put a smile on my face!

With kind regards.
Ann-Marie Cooper, Parliamentary Asst to Ms Alexander MSP

From: Rosemary Hannay [mailto:hannayrosemary@hotmail.com]
Sent: 13 September 2001 16:26
To:wendy.alexander.msp@scottish.parliament.uk
Subject: FAO ANNE-MARIE COOPER

Hi Anne-Marie,

Thanks for your e-mail. From what you say I am not quite sure if you want the pics or not? I live in Glasgow and will be quite happy to drive to wherever your meeting is and drop off the incriminating evidence.

After I wrote to Wendy I had a trawl through my old stuff and have come across even more exotic examples of the Sunday Mail's political editor in compromising positions. Several show him wearing nothing but his socks and have been shot from 'interesting' angles!! Let me know where to drop them off and I'll deliver them under brown paper cover tout de suite.

Dr. Rosemary Hannay

PS. Any chance of a normal photo of Wendy for my daughter Amelia (10)?

From: Wendy.Alexander.msp@scottish.parliament.uk
To: hannayrosemary@hotmail.com
Subject: RE: FAO Anne-Marie Cooper
Sent: Mon, 17 Sep 2001 16:03

Hi Dr Hannay

I don't think Wendy wanted to actually see the pics – by the sounds of things, she thought they would be better off not seen!! I will get a lovely picture of her sent off to you.
Thanks.

Ann-Marie

From: Rosemary Hannay
To: Anne-Marie Cooper
Subject: Pants
Sent: Mon, 17 Sep 2001

Hi Anne-Marie,

Thanks for offering to send a photo for my daughter.

I have come across another old snap of Lindsay posing in nothing but a vest and socks!! There are some things a woman 'Shouldn't ought to see.' He is holding my cat Sooki and looking 'small' and vulnerable if you know what I mean. That's one of the reasons it didn't work out frankly.

I could send it for Wendy's personal collection if she wants!! It would be great if she whipped it out at the next Press Conference and said, 'I found this lying on the floor. . . I'll pass it round to see if any of you recognise it.' Chortle!

Thanks

Dr. Rosemary Hannay

From: Dr Rosemary Hannay
To: Jackie Baillie MSP
Sent: Fri, 17 Aug 2001 11:12
Subject: Tory Hypocrisy

Hi Jackie,

Although now a good Labour party member (12 years) and social liberal, in my youth I consorted with some very dubious elements viz. Young Conservatives. (My parents were putative Tories – 'give me the child till it is seven and I will give you the adult' – to paraphrase the Jesuits.)

A contemporary of mine in Ayrshire in the late seventies was one Philip Gallie. I didn't know him terribly well but we moved in the same political and cultural circles.

To cut a long story short, whilst having some of my old Betamax videos transferred to VHS I came across some 'interesting' footage of young Phil which the present Tory spokesman on 'group sex' might find discomfiting if it entered the public arena.

Jackie you can perhaps appreciate the moral and political dilemma I face. Should I drop the bumptious little twerp in it or should I destroy the incriminating evidence. I have struggled mightily with this ethical enigma but found it impossible to resolve.

I will be in Edinburgh next Friday and would like to drop a copy of the offending item into your office to see what your advice would be on this delicate subject. Unless I hear from you that it is inconvenient (or you can make a decision without viewing the film) I'll pop through your door about 09:30.

Regards

Dr. Rosemary Hannay

PS. If you are absent can I depend on the discretion of your office staff?

From: Jackie Baillie MSP
To: Rosemary Hannay
Sent: Mon, 27 Aug 2001 12:36
Subject: Tory Hypocrisy

Dear Dr Hannay

Thanks for your e-mail dated 17 August 2001.

The thought of Phil Gallie on film is distinctly unedifying. Without needing to see the material my advice would be not to put this into the public arena. . . after all we were all young once (and foolish).

Regretfully I didn't get this e-mail from my office in time for us to meet, but I hope this has helped you to reach a decision you are comfortable with.

Jackie Baillie MSP
Dumbarton Constituency.

From: Rosemary Hannay
To: Jackie Baillie MSP
Sent: Wed, 30 Aug 2001 11:01
Subject: Tory MSPs

Dear Jackie,

Thanks for your eminently reasonable and morally honest reply to my letter. It's good to see at least one politician is not ready to sink to the lowest depth to cheaply denigrate their political opponents.

Unfortunately I think you must have a snitch in your office because I have been contacted by the Sunday Mail's political editor and he knows all about the video and its contents. He kept demanding 'Have you passed the video to Jackie Baillie?'

In the circumstances I think it best to drop the video into your office next Wednesday and let you deal with the press on this one!

Will that be OK?

Dr Rose Hannay

From: Jackie Baillie MSP
To: Rosemary Hannay
Sent: Mon, 3 Sep 2001 14:50
Subject: Tory MSPs

Dear Dr Hannay

Thank you for your e-mail of 30 August 2001 regarding the video tape you hold in your possession.

I have made enquiries and I can confirm that the leak did not emanate from my office. Only two members of my staff had sight of your e-mail, both have a proven track record of maintaining confidentiality and I have absolutely no doubts whatsoever regarding their integrity and discretion.

If you have sought advice elsewhere in this connection you may wish to explore the possibility of the leak emanating from there.

While your correspondence is unclear about the nature of the material on tape, I am sure that you will appreciate that it would be inappropriate for me to take possession of the tape and I have absolutely no desire to view its contents, benign or otherwise.

I note your desire to counter Phil Gallie's argument and expose any hypocrisy that may exist. Ultimately, however, this is a matter for you to decide upon and my advice remains as I stated in my previous e-mail.

I am grateful that you saw fit to bring this matter to my attention and I hope that you are able to come to a decision that you are comfortable with.

Yours sincerely

Jackie Baillie MSP
Dumbarton Constituency

From: Archie Beatty [mailto:snash@maxies.fsnet.co.uk]
Sent: 11 May 2001 11:08
To: Sarah.Boyack.msp@scottish.parliament.uk
Subject: Underground

Hi Sarah,

I am a 75-year-old Labour party supporter from Govan. My good lady wife and I use the underground almost everyday. I am shocked to see from my Scotsman this morning that the EEC has ordered the privatisation of our wee 'clockwork orange'.

I see you are quoted as saying you have no plans to privatise it but that's what Mr Prescott said about air traffic control (Our Air is Not For Sale) before the last election and what Mr Blunkett said about education. 'Watch my lips, no selection,' he said. (I thought it was poignant that he was the only one in the whole hall who couldn't see his lips.)

My neighbour John next door says you're all the same and that's it now; the underground will be privatised. John is a bit of a Nat. How can I convince him that you won't do a Prescott after the elections?

Yours Sincerely
Archie Beatty

PS. This is my first ever e-mail my grand-daughter Amelia has helped me.

From: Johanne.Eady@scottish.parliament.uk on behalf of Sarah.Boyack.MSP
To: Archie Beatty
Sent: Fri, 11/05/01 12:27

Dear Mr Beatty

Thank you for your e-mail – we are pleased to be the recipients of your first ever e-mail! I have forwarded your message on to the Scottish Executive for a fuller reply, but wanted to let you know that the Scottish Executive has absolutely no plans to privatise the Glasgow Underground. The European Commission is at the early stages of preparing a transport regulation but it is at very early stages. The Scottish Executive will be able to give you further detail.

Yours sincerely
Jo Eady

From: Archie Beatty
To: Johanne.Eady@scottish.parliament.uk
Sent: Fri, 11/05/01 14:41
Subject: Underground

Hi Jo,

We were thrilled to get an e-mail from the Minister for Transport so quickly. We don't want to be any bother and have heard that questions to the Executive are costing a fortune. So don't send our message to the Exec. Just get Sarah to drop us a wee line saying she won't do a Prescott so I can show it to John next door.

Could you clear something up for Mrs Beatty? I say that Sarah has adopted that rather unflattering puritan, pudding-head hairdo because she has always got her cycle helmet on her napper. The wife says it is because she is a busy top class politician who hasn't the time to bother with her appearance. Who's right?

Archie and Sadie Beatty

Don't Vote for an Idiot, Vote for a Clown

101 Boghall St.
Moodiesburn
Glasgow G69 1DS

Wed. 31 July 2002

Robert Brown MSP
The Scottish Parliament
Edinburgh EH99 1SP

Dear Robert,

A scandalous article appeared today in the 'Scottish Daily Mail' by the egregious ex-editor of 'The Scotsman' Tim Luckhurst. The piece is a sustained and vituperative assault on our party and on Jim (Wallace) in particular. He quotes from a rather unfortunate interview Donald Gorrie MSP gave to Newsnight Scotland, 'Wallace is not really that keen on closing Peterhead Prison, nor on the prison privatisation for which he has been ridiculed'. If this is true Luckhurst splutters then, 'Wallace has less backbone than a jelly fish.' Luckhurst then monotonously ridicules Jim Wallace as, 'naive . . . spectacularly inept. . . fictional buffoon. . . Homer Simpson . . . Rowan Atkinson's Mr Bean. . . pantomime horse. . . obedient poodle'.

The following paragraph is particularly offensive. 'This is the man who was prepared to back Henry McLeish when McLeish himself had already decided to quit. If Labour had not explained the situation in words of one syllable, it is likely that Jim Wallace QC, MSP, would have voted in favour of a disgraced First Minister who had shamed Scotland.'

Robert, isn't this exactly the 'bitch journalism' Lord Steel has so rightly condemned? We can expect this kind of coruscating invective from New Labour apparatchiks and fellow travellers to reach a crescendo in the run-up to the election. My question to you Robert is how much of this can we take and still remain in the putrefying embrace of these New Labour reptiles?

Yours Sincerely
Asinder Khan

The Scottish Parliament
Robert Brown MSP for Glasgow

REB/MSP/AN/PA

15th August 2002

Mr Asinder Khan
101 Boghall St.
Moodiesbum
Glasgow G69 1DS

Dear Mr Khan,

Thank you for your letter of 31st July 2002. I certainly sympathise and agree with you with your comments about the press as it happens. I am fairly certain that Tim Luckhurst is Conservative rather than the New Labour and certainly his wife stood for the Conservative Party at a by-election.

More worrying is the sort of article we have seen in the last few days in the Daily Record and Daily Mirror attacking Ross Finnie but these tend to be Labour leaning newspapers.

The only answer I can give you is that it does appear that our opinion poll ratings are holding up and that the public do recognise the competence of the Liberal Democrat Ministers and our participation in the Executive and are able to separate it out from the problems of New Labour.

Best Wishes
Robert E Brown MSP
Liberal Democrat MSP for Glasgow

101 Boghall St.
Moodiesburn
Glasgow G69 1DS

27 Aug 02

Robert Brown MSP
The Scottish Parliament
Edinburgh
EH99 1SP

Dear Robert,

Many thanks for your reply of the 15th inst.

I entirely endorse your comments about the 'monstering' Jim and Ross have been getting from the reptiles at 'The Record'. That was my point. While we lodge our snouts half way up New Labours fundament we can expect nothing else.

Robert, can I raise a personal matter with you. I hope you will accept the following in the comradely spirit in which it is offered. Robert, you come across on TV as a little dull and ponderous. No doubt your legal training. Try and speed up your delivery to avoid the tedious monotone that works so well in the courtroom but implies feeblemindedness on the telly.

Your other problem is the eccentric hairstyle. Of course, like me, you are follicly challenged and the temptation to 'comb over' is almost irresistible. But you just look like Gregor Fisher's baldy man ludicrously trying to cover a desiccated dome with an inadequate lock of hair.

My advice is – do a Kinnock!! Have a short back and sides. Get rid of the camouflage. It worked for the Welsh windbag, it will work for you. Jim Wallace won't be there for ever. The Lib Dems will need people of your intelligence and brio. Talk faster and get a sensible haircut and you will go all the way to the top. Drop me a line to say you haven't taken offence at my candid words.

Yours Sincerely
Asinder Khan

The Scottish Parliament
Robert Brown MSP for Glasgow

REB/MSP/AN/PA

10th September 2002

Mr Asinder Khan
101 Boghall St.
Moodiesbum
Glasgow G69 1DS

Dear Asinder,

Thank you for your letter of 27th August 2002 with your candid comments, I am now off on a confidence rebuilding course! No offence taken however.

Best Wishes
Robert E Brown MSP
Liberal Democrat MSP for Glasgow

Don't Vote for an Idiot, Vote for a Clown

From: hannayrosemary@hotmail.com
To: dennis.canavan@scottish.parliament.uk
Subject: small parties rights
Date: Wed, 8 Aug 2001 14:21

Hello Dennis,

I am laid up in hospital (after a climbing accident) with my lap top and catching up on my reading. I see from the Herald that you are standing up for the rights of small parties. Well done.

I wanted to ask you about the future of one very small party viz. Yourself. We were all ecstatic when you won in 1999 and rubbed that ridiculous article Dewar's nose in it. But what does the future hold for you? Surely the next time you will go down to ignominious defeat at the hands of the political pygmies of Blairism?

I know you will keep them guessing till the end but perhaps now is the time to clamber aboard a passing political ship and really shock the philistines.

Drop me a line if you have a second. I'd love to be able to say I had corresponded with the MSP with the biggest one in the Parliament – majority that is!!

Dr Rose Hannay

FROM THE OFFICE OF DENNIS CANAVAN
MSP FOR FALKIRK WEST

Dear Dr Hannay,

Thank you for your e-mail asking after Dennis. I am sorry to learn of your incapacity at this time – I hope the food is not too unbearable!!

Unfortunately, Dennis is on holiday at the moment and, therefore, is unable to reply at this time. However, I shall forward your communication to the constituency office for his attention and he shall contact you upon his return.

Best wishes for a speedy recovery,
Yours sincerely Maureen H Conner
Parliamentary Assistant to Dennis Canavan MSP

From: dennis-canavan@constituencyoffice.freeserve.co.uk
To: hannayrosemary@hotmail.com
Subject: small parties rights
Date: Fri, 24 August 2001 09:54

Dear Rose

Thank you for your e-mail message of 8 August.

I am sorry to hear about your climbing accident and I hope that you are now back home from hospital.

At present, I have no intention of joining any political party but I do not share your prophecy of ignominious defeat. I am surprised to hear such pessimism from a climber, albeit an injured one, and I do hope that you have a speedy and full recovery.

With best wishes
Dennis Canavan MSP

From: hannayrosemary@hotmail.com
To: dennis.canavan.msp@scottish.parliament.uk
Subject: small parties rights
Date: Sat, 25 August 2001 09:51

Hi Dennis,

Thanks for the e-mail. Dennis, there are two great pitfalls in politics, one is self delusion the other is obstinacy. After your inexplicable attempts to rejoin New Labour and your equally inexplicable (and frankly Dennis, ludicrous) decision to take the 'cream puff' you have been reduced to a figure of fun.

Whenever your name is mentioned in our staffroom the Blairites start singing 'he put his left leg in, he put his left leg out, in out, in out, shake it all about'. It is a little humiliating for those of us who lauded you as a principled left critic of New Labour to see you revealed as a dithering nincompoop.

You say you do not share my 'prophecy of ignominious defeat'. There are none so blind as those who will not see! And you are so blinkered you could be running in the 4:30 at Ayr. Ask your friends if you can win next time? If they are honest they will tell you straight that you have as much chance as an ice lolly in Hades.

But all is not lost if you take decisive action now. Here is what I propose. (It's a bit shocking but hear me through before throwing one of your characteristic wobblies.)

Join the Tories, Dennis!!

They defend the same policies as New Labour who you were going to join, PFI, vouchers for Asylum seekers, brown-nosing press Barons etc. and your difficult personality will not be a block to promotion in that party of nutters. What do you say? I think it is an inspired piece of Machiavellian duplicity. No one will see it coming. The alternative is joining the Greens – a dispiriting prospect I'm sure you'll agree. (Bad enough sitting on the same row as headbanger Harper without having to call him comrade, eh?)

Let me have your thoughts on this, Dennis. Don't be afraid to be brutally frank. But remember I have plaster casts on both legs already!

Rosemary Hannay

From: dennis-canavan@constituencyoffice.freeserve.co.uk
To: hannayrosemary@hotmail.com
Subject: small parties rights
Date: Tues, 4 Sep 2001 14:31

Dear Rose

Are you sure it's just your legs that are plastered?
Get well soon!

Dennis

101 Boghall St.
Moodiesburn
Glasgow G69 1DS

20/05/02

Dear Cathy,

I am sure you saw Robbie Dinwoodie's mischievous and garbled report in last Friday's Herald. He reproduced the Keir Hardie quotation,viz. 'The toady who crawls through the mire of self-abasement to enable him/her to bask in the smile of royalty is a victim of a diseased organism.'

He ridiculed you for presuming to pontificate on whether Croy Celtic Supporters Club (CCSC) would join you in 'congratulating the Queen on her Golden Jubilee.' He then scoffed at the idea that such a body could be 'a bastion of royalism'. Indeed he even questioned whether the CCSC existed, implying that you had dissembled in the parliament. I hope you have fired off a blistering reply to this poison dwarf.

Shamefully, I have to admit I had never heard of Keir Hardie before. I got his biography from the library. As you know he was the founder of the Party. In 1893 he 'protested against parliamentary time being wasted on a motion of congratulation at the Duke of York's marriage'.

In 1894 on a resolution for 'an humble Address' of congratulation to the royal couple on the birth of the baby who became Edward VIII (the Nazi sympathiser) he said, '. . . in the interests of the dignity of the House I take leave to protest. . . from his childhood onward this boy will be surrounded by sycophants and flatterers by the score.'

This 'Royal Baby speech' was seen as scandalous and marked him out as the Sheridan of his day. Hardie's protest was solitary. My question is Did Mr Keir Hardie go too far? Should he have been ignored as you recommended in this case? Or do you think that in the conditions then, criticism of an undemocratic, mediaeval oligarchy was justified, but no longer?

I profess I am mystified.

Yours Sincerely
Asinder Khan

101 Boghall St.
Moodiesburn
Glasgow G69 1DS

04/07/02

Dear Cathy,

I wrote to you on the 20/05/02 but have not had a reply. I assume my correspondence has been mislaid. (I include a copy of the original.)

However the substance of my letter, viz. that you lied in the parliament about the existence of the Croy Celtic Supporters club (CCSC) has played on my mind ever since. The probity and veracity of an MSP is jealously guarded. Once sullied it is lost forever.

I will be in Edinburgh a week this Friday. I intend to handcuff myself to the doors of the building which houses the MSPs offices. I have made a large banner from a sheet which says in red, 'Cathy Craigie is no liar, Croy Celtic Supporters Club exists and is Loyal.' I will remain chained to the doors until Dinwoodie issues a correction and apology. I will phone the BBC and STV just in advance to make sure of good coverage. My daughter, Chitra, is a researcher on the Lesley Riddoch Programme.

Cathy, can I tell them I have your support on this?

Yours Sincerely
Asinder Khan

Cathie Craigie MSP
The Scottish Parliament
Edinburgh EH99 1SP

09 July 2002

Dear Asinder,

Thank you for your letter of 4 July. I appreciate you sending me a copy of your original letter of 20 May as I did not receive it.

I can only assume that the Herald misheard my comments in the Scottish Parliament on the 16 May. I have enclosed a copy of the Parliament's Official Report for your information.

While I appreciate the sentiments in your letter and your concern in politics we have to accept comment and humour in the vein that it is intended.

Yours sincerely

Cathie Craigie MSP

Don't Vote for an Idiot, Vote for a Clown

From: Rosemary Hannay [mailto:hannayrosemary@hotmail.com]
Sent: 24 September 2001 21:47
To: roseanna.cunningham.msp@scottish.parliament.uk
Subject: TV Appearance

Hello Roseanna,

I just thought I'd drop you a line to say how impressed I was with your speech on Prisons to the Conference. Succinctly delivered, with great authority. I got the very strong sense that you are destined to lead the Party into the next General Election. Although I have enormous respect for John I feel he hasn't the passion or energy (now he has take up with Ms. Quigley) to prosecute the fight.

Can I, at the risk of provoking offence and as an older Party member, offer you a little advice? Always keep your styling mousse handy if you're going on TV Roseanna!! You obviously have the same kind of hair as me and I'm afraid it was rather standing up when you were at the podium. (My husband said you looked like a startled 'lavvy brush' but he is no oil painting himself.) He noted the slogan was 'We staun fur Scotland' and quipped 'she's taken that too far noo'.

The thought of a woman First Minister is very exciting! Please drop me a brief line to say you haven't taken umbrage at the ravings of an old woman.

Dr. Rosemary Hannay
(Silver surfer)

From: Roseanna.Cunningham.msp@scottish.parliament.uk
To: hannayrosemary@hotmail.com
Subject: RE: TV Appearance
Date: Tues, 25 Sep 2001 11:57

My hair is a perpetual problem – but this may just be a generational thing you know. I have never been keen on very styled hair and do in fact prefer to keep mine on the slightly spiky side.

If I was 30 years younger I might have been a punk. So you see, it might have been a great deal worse!

Roseanna

From: Rosemary Hannay [mailto:hannayrosemary@hotmail.com]
Sent: 17 September 2001 08:29
To: susan.deacon.msp@scottish.parliament.uk
Subject: Lesley Riddoch

Hi Susan,

I heard you on the Lesley Riddoch show on Friday and thought you superb, as usual. Riddoch was her predictable, patronising, snide self. I detest the woman. She is a dyed in the wool Nationalist. However you made short work of her incoherent carping.

After the programme a few of us in the Nursing Home had a chin wag about your ideas on efficiency in the NHS. You said if it works and it is efficient then it should be employed in the Health service. I totally agree with you.

Amelia, who has the next room to me, argued that on that basis there was no ideological reason not to return the whole NHS to the private sector as long as it worked and could be shown to work. She quoted the French system. I said that was indeed the rationale in the present trajectory of the Government's stewardship of the National Health Service. Amelia is a bit old Labour and said that such an outcome would be a shameful negation of all our generation had fought for. Silly old fool!

As long as I get my hip replacements I don't care if Coca Cola finance the operation or Mr Branson makes a few bob from the transaction.

Susan, am I on the right track on this one? I would hate to be thought old fashioned or out of date. (Although, I am 82.) I know you are a very busy girl but it would make this 'silver surfer's' day to get an e-mail from the horse's mouth!!

Regards

Dr. Rosemary Hannay

From: Susan.Deacon.msp@scottish.parliament.uk
To: hannayrosemary@hotmail.com
Subject: RE: Lesley Riddoch
Date: Wed, 19 Sep 2001 11:25

Rosemary

Thank you for your email. It is good to hear that the Health Service debate goes on at the 'front line'! and I am pleased to hear that you and I are in agreement.

Thanks again for taking the time to let me have your thoughts on this – it was much appreciated.

Yours
Susan Deacon

From: hannayrosemary@hotmail.com
To: susan.deacon.msp@scottish.parliament.uk
Subject: Kennel Club
Date: 16 Sep 01

Hello Susan,

My wife and I are labour party members in Livingston.

I presume the MSP doesn't actually read the e-mails.

We have just been given a puppy by our daughter. She is an eight week old Char-Pei. She is very feisty, indeed irrationally aggressive, and yesterday bit our postman on the unmentionables.

Do you think Susan would mind if we named the dog after her. It will go on the kennel club certificate and it would be the full name – Susan Deacon MSP.

Hope that will be all right?

Philip Hannay

Dorothy-Grace and the police horses

From: Rosemary Hannay hannayrosemary@hotmail.com
Sent: 08 August 2001 15:53
To: dorothy.elder.msp@scottish.parliament.uk
Subject: Govanhill Pool

Dear Dorothy-Grace,

I see from the papers that you have been facing down police horses outside Govanhill pool. Well done. I dare say the cuddies were quivering at the sight of you in high dudgeon. I know I would.

I remember you from the days of the co-operative. It's good to see some people still have a social conscience and haven't lost their principles (or cojones)! More than could be said for some in the Party. (I don't trust that Mike Russell, patronising big English balloon, (I know I shouldn't say it but. . .). The day we see John Swinney face up to Polis horses and riot police is the day I'll eat my beret!!

I am laid up in Hospital (after a climbing accident – I tried to get the whisky from the top cupboard) with my lap top and my neighbour says she met you at a meeting on MS. Just to let you know we are with you spiritually (as we'd be bugger all use physically). All the best from Marie in the next bed and me viz.

Dr. Rosemary Hannay

PS. If you could drop us a wee line it would be great, the wee nurses don't believe we sent you an e-mail.

From: Dorothy Elder MSP
To: Hannayrosemary
Sent: Thurs, 09 Aug 2001 15:31
Subject: RE Govanhill Pool

Just read this message, so sorry to hear about your accident. Get in touch soon.

Dorothy-Grace

From: Rosemary Hannay [mailto:hannayrosemary@hotmail.com]
Sent: 09 August 2001 11:09
To: dorothy.elder.msp@scottish.parliament.uk
Subject: baths

Dorothy-Grace,

Hi, it's us again. We saw your letter in the Herald this morning and it was spot on. Only one weakness in your reasoning. You say 'there was special need for police elsewhere'.

The flaw in this is that in Sighthill they need CID and undercover special units. The bog-standard plods used at Govanhill are well known as bigoted racist scum and so their deployment in Sighthill would certainly have been disastrous.

Did you notice the snippet in the story on page 6 where Police 'denied that the Herald photo of mounted officers among the crowd showed they had been heavy-handed'. We have yesterday's Herald here and you can see at least 4 horses trampling people. Is that you under the grey one?

Dr. Rose Hannay and Marie (ward 6)

From: Dorothy-Grace Elder MSP
To: HannayRosemary
Sent: Thurs, 09 Aug 2001 15:29
Subject: RE: Baths

Many thanks for your email. I appreciate that CID must do the Sighthill job but making the point police needed there was important in public terms.

With very best wishes,
Dorothy-Grace

Dorothy-Grace and the back stabbers

From: Rosemary Hannay
To: Dorothy-Grace Elder MSP
Sent: Wed, 19 Sep 2001 10:10
Subject: Back-Stabbers

Hi Dorothy-Grace,

I saw the outrageous article by Dumbwoodie in this morning's Herald and I wanted to write to you immediately to express my support and solidarity. The back-stabbers have certainly scented blood. By accusing you of failing to pay the 5000 pounds into central party funds for the second year they hope to smear you as unstable and rapacious. A poisonous combination. They then throw in stories of a 'public falling out with one of her own staff' implying that you are a difficult eccentric! (I met Fiona MacAulay down at Gartocher Terrace, when the stone-mad residents were fighting with the Police every day. She was a bonnie big lass but I fear a 'bear of very little brain'. I presume this became all too evident when you started to work with her.)

Dorothy-Grace can I as an independent observer, sympathetic to you, offer some unbiased advice? You are quoted as retorting to the accusations 'This is just the usual pile of poo-poo.' You also say there is a 'whispering campaign' against you by 'the usual suspects.' Dorothy-Grace it is with trepidation that I have to tell you that bizarre, infantile phraseology like 'pile of poo-poo' makes you sound loopy, and greetin' about 'whispering campaigns' makes you appear loopy and paranoid.

If it's crap say it's crap and if Kay Ullrich is a back-stabbing, adenoidal, nonentity say so. Call a spade a spade. You are no shrinking violet in your journalism so don't let being an MSP atrophy your brain. Please let me know that you have not taken offence at my candid comments.

Best Regards
Dr. Rosemary Hannay

Don't Vote for an Idiot, Vote for a Clown

From: Dorothy-Grace Elder MSP
To: Dr. Rosemary Hannay
Sent: Mon, 22 Oct 2001 14:19
Subject: Dorothy-Grace Elder MSP

Hi Rosemary

Dorothy-Grace is very keen to speak with you. Can you give us a contact telephone number.
We have found your emails very amusing and Dorothy-Grace extends her apologies for the late reply.

Evelyn McKechnie
Parliamentary Researcher to Dorothy-Grace Elder, MSP

From: Rosemary Hannay hannayrosemary@hotmail.com
Sent: 31 October 2001 10:57
To: d.g.e.msp@btclick.com
Subject: Ship of Fools

Hi Evelyn,

Thanks for your e-mails. Please tell Dorothy-Grace that I appreciate her gesture but I know she is desperately busy and she shouldn't feel she has to respond to my rambling missives.

I noted from the Sunday Times that the scurrilous whispering campaign rumbles forward. The ST reported that Swinney (that peally wally vampire) physically ejected Dorothy-Grace from his office and allowed himself to use profanities. Next time I meet John at conference I intend to inform him that he is nothing but a foul mouthed, knuckle-dragging, two-faced, speccy, misogynous bampot!!

They also reported that Dorothy-Grace was in secret talks with Tommy Sheridan about 'jumping the dyke'. They say she baulked at having to live on a worker's wage. Once again they sinisterly attempt to smear her as a venal, disloyal, screwball.

Tell D-G 'Don't let the Bastards get you down.'

Regards
Rosemary Hannay

PS. I take it that Dorothy-Grace isn't about to jump ship, is she?

From: hannayrosemary@hotmail.com]
Sent: 14 September 2001 10:19
To: alex.fergusson.msp@scottish.parliament.uk
Subject: TV Appearance

Hi Alex,

I saw you being interviewed in the black and white corridor with that waste of space Keith Harding. When Ian MacWhirter asked him 'What were the main themes of the campaign?' he obviously didn't have a clue!!

Is this really the calibre of the IDS troops Alex? Thank God you were there to jump in with a coherent answer or the viewers would have thought all us Conservatives were knuckle-dragging morons like Mr. Harding.

I am house-bound and watch the Holyrood Programme religiously but this is the first time I have come across Keith. Is he entirely pukka? Seems like a flippin' liability to me. A myopic Lib Dem rather than a Tory!! Is our party really going to be torn in two by political pygmies of Mr Harding's ilk?

Am I being too hard on the wee man?

Regards
Dr. Rosemary Hannay

From: hannayrosemary@hotmail.com
To: Keith.Harding.msp@scottish.parliament.uk
Subject: TV Appearance
Date: Fri, 14 Sep 2001 10:51

Hello Keith,

I saw you being interviewed on TV yesterday in the Parliament with that knuckle-dragging moron Alex Fergusson. I'm glad to see an IDS supporter get on the Holyrood programme at last.

I was sorry to see you rather discombobulated when that New Labour sycophant Ian McWhirter asked you a trick question viz. What were the main themes of the leadership campaign? A deceptively simply inquiry but devilishly hard to field if you don't know.

Beardy Fergusson butted in making a fellow Conservative look a little credulous. Whose side is he on? I fear that this is only the thin edge of a very thick wedge. Don't let Kenneth Clarke's political thugs push you around.

Regards
Dr. Rosemary Hannay

PS. IDS is widely reputed to be a hanger and a flogger, as I am myself. Where do you stand on these important questions Keith?

From: Alex.Fergusson.msp@scottish.parliament.uk
To: hannayrosemary@hotmail.com
Subject: RE :TV Appearance
Date: Mon, 17 Sep 2001 18:30

Dear Dr Hannay,

I apologise for taking so long to reply to your e-mail, but I was out of contact over the weekend. I have discovered since last Thursday that my colleague had not appeared on live television before, and I suspect that the occasion got to him. He is as hard a worker as the rest of us with long experience of local government which is very useful to us as a group.

I sincerely hope that we will not be 'torn in two', as you put it, for if we are we will be finished as a credible party. As a Ken Clark supporter, I await with interest to see how IDS goes about his difficult task, and he will have my backing as he does so. He has to prove himself a heavyweight, and I hope that he does so. The alternative is too grim to contemplate.

Thank you again for your kind remarks (about me at any rate!)

Yours sincerely,

Alex Ferguson

From: hannayrosemary@hotmail.com
To: Alex.fergusson.msp@scottish.parliament.uk
Subject: Numpties
Date: Fri, 28 Sep 2001 10:42

Hi Alex,

I was flabbergasted to learn that Keith Harding has been an MSP for 2 years and had never been on TV before. Hells Bells, Alex what has the idiot been up to all this time? Our group really are a bunch of useless 'Merchant Bankers'.

John Scott was interviewed by McWhirter on the Holyrood Programme yesterday and bugger me if he didn't dry up as well!! Do you have to be a myopic moron to be a Conservative MSP or does it just help? I despair of the whole cretinous crew. The only one who impresses (and is a potential rival to you for the leadership, Alex) is David Davidson. He has poise, style and elegance. Although, I hear rumours of indolence!!

Contrast this inertia with your prodigious work-rate. You are never off the box! BSE, Foot and Mouth, Fox Hunting, you are ineffably there with a ready, pithy quote indicting the Government. You have only one Achilles heel. Can I speak freely Alex?

The beard!! My husband often shouts through to the kitchen 'Here's that MSP you like on TV'. I cry 'Which one?' 'The one that looks like an armpit with eyes!' Hirsuteness is for wild boar, chimps and circus performers not for aspiring Tory statesmen. Lose the facial fluff and the world is your lobster or remain on the back benches with the rest of the mediocre scruffbags.

Seek the advice of Annabel Goldie. It was eccentric old trouts like her who delivered the election for that antediluvian no-hoper IDS!

Ask her how she feels about a great set of hairy chops breathing down her back on the Tory benches. With some distaste I'll be bound. Keep Annabel sweet and McLetchie's job is yours.

Dr. Rosemary Hannay

PS. Rereading this I hope my candour hasn't caused offence. Please drop me a line to say that you haven't taken umbrage at my comradely advice?

101 Boghall St.
Moodiesburn
Glasgow G69 1DS

30/05/02

My Dear Mr. Fitzpatrick,

In your letter to the Scotsman newspaper last Tuesday you said,
'I wholly disagree with and reject the identity politics of
Salmon, Swinney and co, but I do not equiponderate them with
the hatreds and racism at the core of Le Pen's creed.'

My computer spell-check had never heard of the word
'equiponderate'.

I confess I had to go to the reference library to discover the
meaning. (The insolent librarian who consulted the O.E.D. for
me averred that anyone employing such verbosity in a daily
newspaper was a 'verbal dandy'. Cheeky blighter! I told him you
were an MSP and therefore professionally impelled to a certain
prolixity.)

I had just instructed my Higher Still class to read the
broadsheets to improve their vocabulary when your excellent
letter appeared and I was able to send them scurrying to the
dictionaries and thesauri.

Could I prevail on you to recommend five books they could read
which would help them to aspire to the wordsmanship and
eloquence which you have mastered?

Yours Sincerely

Asinder Khan

PS. They have already perused Robert Tressell's 'Ragged
Trousers. . .'

Please reply to Constituency Office:
2 Canniesburn Toll
Bearsden

24 January 2003

Asinder Khan
47 Penzance Way
Moodiesbum G69 OPD

Dear Mr Khan

You wrote to me as long ago as 30 May 2002 (copy letter enclosed for ease of reference). I am very sorry that you have not received a reply from me. Your letter seems to have been caught up in another bundle of correspondence and only now has it come to my attention.

I must make a confession: In my own letter I had used the legal term equiparate and it seems to have been the Scotsman's own spell check or sub-editors who substituted 'equiponderate'. I did know that it was a word, but it is not one that I would normally have used.

I certainly could recommend five books, but I am not sure that your pupils would readily set to reading them. I don't think anyone who loves words could escape having a sound grasp of both the Bible and the complete works of Shakespeare. I was, incidentally, delighted to see that they were familiar with Robert Tressell.

I am not so sure about eloquence on my part, but I would suggest that the following might be recommended to your students:

1) Anything by Thomas Hardy, with my own favourite being Jude the Obscure. When stuck, I am always drawn to his poem, 'On a Fine Moming'.

2) Balzac, who famously remarked that 'I am not deep, but very wide', and my own favourite is Cousin Bette.

3) For an example of work that demonstrates the benefit of working through the complexity of language, I can think of no

better than Gerard Manley Hopkins who of course spent some time in Glasgow and whose use of language and rhyme is difficult at the outset but rewards perseverance. I find it difficult to point out one favourite, but would mention 'God's Grandeur', 'Hurrahing in Harvest', 'No Worst, There is None', and 'The Windhover'.

4) I would recommend anything by John Keats. I think he has a freshness of phrase and a quick but extensive imagination which repays reading. Again it is difficult to pick out any one piece, but perhaps 'Hyperion'?

5) Finally, I think it might be helpful to mention a poet whose use of simple language still manages to communicate deep themes and a personal favourite of mine is Robert Frost. His collection, 'A Boy's Will' is one I often dig out with my own favourite being 'A Late Walk'.

I hope you find these thoughts helpful and that they might be of some assistance to your class.

Thank you for writing to me.

Yours sincerely
BRIAN FITZPATRICK MSP
Working for the people of Strathkelvin and Bearsden

101 Boghall St.
Moodiesburn
Glasgow G69 1DS

30 Jan. 03

Brian Fitzpatrick MSP
2 Canniesburn Toll
Bearsden
Glasgow G61 2QU

My Dear Mr Fitzpatrick,

I thank you for the astonishingly tardy reply to my letter.

You are quite right, your book recommendations are quite unsuitable. I was hoping you would suggest things like 'The Valley of the Dolls', 'American Psycho' or Burroughs' 'The Naked Lunch'.

Keats? Gerald Manley Hopkins? For crying out loud!?! What about Trainspotting, Adrian Mole, Bill Bryson - not Thomas bleedin' Hardy?

Yours Etc.
Asinder Khan

PS. I was flabbergasted to see that you finished your missive with the slogan, 'Working for the people of Strathkelvin and Bearsden'. Your constituents are up in arms campaigning to 'Save Stobhill Hospital' while you are conniving to shut it. You bounder! I joined a march and rally last Saturday in Bearsden attended by 300 of your elderly constituents. Every malady known to medical science was represented and they were baying for your blood. You were denounced by every imprecation imaginable except curiously – as a poseur!

From: Archie Beatty [mailto:snash@maxies.fsnet.co.uk]
Sent: 10 May 2001 11:10
To: phil.gallie.msp@scottish.parliament.uk
Subject: Videos

Hi Phil,

I see from my Herald this morning that your irrepressible exuberance has got you in hot water again. Hope you don't have to pull them down.

Phil, like you in my youth I was a member of the SNP. I've had some of my old Beta Max videos transferred to VHS and have uncovered some 'interesting' footage of Mike Russell MSP dancing at a fund raising party in the seventies.

As the Tory spokesman on group sex I think you should have a look at this. I will be in Edinburgh next Friday and will drop a copy into your office.

Yours Etc.
Archie Beatty

From: Phil.Gallie.msp@scottish.parliament.uk
Sent: Fri. 11/05/01 09:10
To: 'Archie Beatty'
Subject: RE: Videos

Thanks for the offer. Accepted albeit the fact that I was not a member of the SNP in my youth may influence your thinking. In my youth I am not sure if the SNP existed!

Happy to say South Ayrshire Council recognised their failure to communicate. They have reviewed the position and there is no requirement for us to remove any of our posters. The real problem was lack of ambition by the other parties in my view.

Phil

From: Archie Beatty [mailto:snash@maxies.fsnet.co.uk]
Sent: 11 May 2001 10:02
To: Phil.Gallie@scottish.parliament.uk
Subject: Naked truth

Hi Phil,

Thanks for your e-mail and I will look forward to meeting you in the flesh next Friday morning.

Just a thought, have you got a video player in your office? Also you might want to give any young female secretaries the morning off as the video has some pretty torrid scenes before our friend Russell bursts on to the screen.

Mrs Beatty and I agree that you may want to look into the legal implications of this before I arrive, we don't all want to end up in a private prison over the first Holyrood sex scandal.

See you Friday!

Yours Etc.
Archie Beatty

From: Phil.Gallie.msp@scottish.parliament.uk
Sent: Mon. 14/05/01 09:42
To: 'Archie Beatty'
Subject: Naked Truth

No we do not have a video mc in Office. I was not aware of your imminent arrival. I will discuss.

Phil

Copy to Pat please Susan.

Dear Archie
On checking my diary, I see that Friday morning has been otherwise booked. I have no note of arrangements for the meeting you refer to in your message. Please forward the video to me and I will look at it.

Yours sincerely
Phil Gallie

From: Archie Beatty
Sent: Mon. 14/05/01 19:05
To: Phil.Gallie.msp@scottish.parliament.uk
Subject: Naked Truth

Dear Phil,

You must be joking !! I'm not sending this through the mail. You, Mrs Beatty and me might end up on the Sex Offenders Register.

I'll bring it in as agreed on Friday under brown paper cover. If you could arrange to have a mature and responsible person take delivery. We don't want some young rascal making copies and it ending up as a fund raising tool at Conservative Association functions.

If you could spare a few minutes yourself I would love to take you by the mitt.

Yours Etc.
Archie Beatty

From: hannayrosemary@hotmail.com
Sent: 17 September 2001 15:26
To: kenneth.gibson.msp@scottish.parliament.uk
Subject: Request to appear on TV

Hi Kenny,

I am putting together an advertising campaign for the Scottish Meat Marketing Board and we would like to recruit two or three MSPs for TV adverts. The idea is to show a short clip of Henry McLeish speaking then cut to an MSP who will shout:–

'The First Minister is talking MINCE' (cut to FM again then back to MSP) 'Scottish Mince'

Followed by the Board's logo and a voiceover extolling the delights of Scottish Meat Produce.

We understand that payments direct to Parliamentarians would be problematic so we propose to pay the £500 appearance fee to a youth or community group in your constituency. I will write to you formally but could you give me a preliminary indication if this project is something which you would consider?

Regards
Dr. Rosemary Hannay

From: Kenneth.Gibson.msp@scottish.parliament.uk
To: hannayrosemary@hotmail.com
Subject: RE: Request to appear on TV
Date: Tues, 18 Sep 2001 11:01

Yes, why not!
Best regards
Kenneth

Don't Vote for an Idiot, Vote for a Clown

From: hannayrosemary@hotmail.com
To: kenneth.gibson.msp@scottish.parliament.uk
Subject: TV Appearance
Date: Wed, 26 Sep 2001 10:41

Hi Kenny,

Many thanks for your prompt confirmation that you would be willing to consider taking part in our advertising campaign. We will write to you formally shortly.

In the interests of reciprocity we would like to recruit a participant from each of the other parties. Kenny, could you recommend some of your colleagues whom I might contact?

We want MSPs who combine a well-developed sense of the absurd and a clownish innocence. (Although perhaps not Frank McAveety because we want to avoid outright oafishness (joke).)

Exclude women MSPs, (as you know they can be difficult and unreasonable) no MSPs with beards (as they don't come across too well on TV) and no obese or dense MSPs. I know this more or less excludes 90% of the Labour group!!

In short we are searching for someone like you. An MSP who combines rakish good looks with a razor sharp brain and incisive political acumen. I know it is a tall order but there must be some other 'normal' MSPs.

Looking forward to hearing your recommendations.

Regards
Dr. Rosemary Hannay

From: Kenneth Gibson MSP
To: Rosemary Hannay
Subject: RE: TV Appearance
Date: Thurs, 11 Oct 2001 13:45

I am afraid you have me stumped re: members of other parties. Murray Tosh? Jamie Stone? Paul Martin?

Good luck!
Kenneth

From: Rosemary Hannay [mailto:hannayrosemary@hotmail.com]
Sent: 01 November 2001 10:03
To: kenneth.gibson.msp@scottish.parliament.uk
Subject: Yellow Stars

Hi Kenneth,

You will, no doubt, have seen the disgraceful piece by Robbie Dumbwoodie in this morning's Herald. Disturbingly, he smears you by declaring 'He is seen as a bruiser and loose cannon. . .' I have also been informed that you are regularly referred to as 'thuggish' in the Scotsman's parliamentary sketch column.

Your claim that smart cards issued to asylum seekers would be equivalent to the yellow stars which Nazi Germany forced Jewish people to wear is, frankly, preposterous.

I know I said we were looking for MSPs with a 'sense of the absurd' (and you certainly fulfil the second requisite) but we do require a modicum of sense. Reluctantly, we have decided to withdraw our offer to you to appear in our meat commercials. We fear you would give mince a bad name!!

Regards

Dr. Rosemary Hannay

PS. I thought the oafish McAveety was suppose to be your pal? What kind of friend joins the pack kicking a man when he has exposed himself as an idiot?

Don't Vote for an Idiot, Vote for a Clown

From: Kenneth Gibson MSP
To: hannayrosemary
Subject: RE: Yellow Stars
Date: Thurs, 01 Nov 2001 14:21

Thank you for your rather confused memo.

Frank McAveety is a pal. We had lunch today.

The reference you refer to was a reiteration of the comment made by Mohammed Asif, spokesperson for Glasgow's Asylum Seekers. He said on GMS yesterday that is how the new system will make him and fellow Asylum Seekers feel.

You know better of course. . .

From: Rosemary Hannay
To: Kenneth Gibson MSP
Subject: Mince
Date: Fri, 02 Nov 2001 08:15

Hi Kenneth,

I have made a terrible mistake. If Mohammed Asif said it then that's obviously OK. I take it you are still keen to take part in the Mince project?

Sorry
Rosemary Hannay

From: Rosemary Hannay hannayrosemary@hotmail.com
Sent: 07 September 2001 16:11
To: annabel.goldie.msp@scottish.parliament.uk
Subject: smack

Hello Annabel,

So the loony left are to stop us legitimately chastising our youngsters!!

Over my dead body. Annabel, I teach a Salvation Army Sunday school for 8 to 12 year olds. I have often found that a skelp round the back of the napper with a hymn book will restore order where all else has failed.

I heard Phil Gaillie on TV say that a whack with a rolled up magazine could be administered entirely lovingly. Phil reported that he had often been soundly thrashed as a boy and it had not affected him. (A claim that went some way to undermining his original argument.)

Annabel, can we count on you to stand up for the rights of Christians to smack the weans?

Regards
Dr. Rosemary Hannay

PS. Spare the rod and spoil the child, I think the good book says, eh?

From: Annabel Goldie MSP
To: Rosemary Hannay
Sent: Thurs, 13 Sep 2001 09:55
Subject: RE: Smack

Dear Dr Hannay

Thank you very much for your email of 7th September.

I have a very great deal of sympathy with your views. None of us approves of or would endorse excessive physical disciplining of any child. Having said that, it seems to be essential that parents must be left free to chastise children reasonably and under current law it is left to the courts to determine what is reasonable, which I think is entirely appropriate.

That means that any parent or adult who behaves excessively in relation to the administering of chastisement then rightly may expect to be confronted by the legal system and be dealt with accordingly.

I know that my Party has taken a very sceptical view of what the Minister for Justice and Home Affairs proposes and we shall await with interest the final details.

Yours sincerely
Annabel M Goldie MSP

From: Rosemary Hannay hannayrosemary@hotmail.com
Sent: 13 September 2001 16:54
To: annabel.goldie.msp@scottish.parliament.uk
Subject: Thrashing weans

Hi Annabel,

Many thanks for your closely argued e-mail.

I am sure we would all agree that 'excessive physical disciplining' is unacceptable, but what is excessive? My mother after reading a biography of Rose Kennedy (Mother of JFK) not only named a daughter after that matriarch but adopted the habit of whacking her children with wooden coathangers! (Of course at that time my mother was unaware of the wicked political actions and perverse sexual predilictions of the ex-president which were directly a result of his mother's sadistic activities.)

John Fs experience turned him into a priapic lunatic and politician. However, subject to the same physical chastisement, I avoided both sexual and political deviancy. (Although, admittedly, I am a Conservative with a weakness for spanking young boys).

I was much encouraged by your unequivocal declaration that it is 'essential that parents must be left free to chastise children reasonably'. Do you agree that the 'Kennedy Method' using coathangers is reasonable and non-excessive?

Will you say so in the Parliament?

Dr. Rosemary Hannay

From: Annabel Goldie MSP
To: Rosemary Hannay
Sent: Wed, 3 Oct 2001 12:55

Dear Dr Hannay

I thank you for your email of 13th September.

I have to say that I would not support the use of 'hangers' as being a reasonable method of administering chastisement to young children.

The use of the parent's hand in a reasonable and safe manner commensurate with the circumstances requiring chastisement would seem to be preferable.

Yours sincerely
Annabel M Goldie MSP
List Member for the West of Scotland

From: Rosemary Hannay
To: Annabel Goldie MSP
Sent: Wed, 3 Oct 2001 14:21
Subject: Beltin' the Weans

Hello Annabel,

Many thanks for your frank and thought provoking letter. I was surprised to learn that you deprecate the use of wooden coathangers in the 'thrashing of weans'. Surely it is exactly equivalent to that old Scottish implement of chastisement, the tawse?

I cannot believe that you would not favour the reintroduction of that most effective form of corporal punishment. My brother Archie was much on the receiving end of the leather strap when he was a lad and it made a man of him! (Unfortunately, he has been held at Her Majesty's pleasure in Peterhead for the last 5 years – embezzlement.)

The only way to deal with football hooligans, Globalisation protesters and Big Issue sellers (i.e. aggressive beggars) is to bring back the belt, the birch and the Rope. Let's see them daub graffiti on the sides of houses or sneer at you for not buying a copy of their tedious magazine after fifty rapid on the bare buttocks. The Swine!!

Sorry, Annabel, I got carried away there for a minute. But I very strongly feel that we are too wishy washy these days and that true Conservative values require robust measures.

Let me know what you think about the reintroduction of the belt?

Regards
Dr. Rosemary Hannay

NO REPLY

Gorrie and the prods

From: Archie Beatty [mailto:snash@maxies.fsnet.co.uk]
Sent: 08 May 2001 14:31
To: donald.gorrie.msp@scottish.parliament.uk
Subject: Sectarianism

Hi Donald,

Can I congratulate you on your commendable initiative on catholic sectarianism. I recently met you at the cartoon show in Edinburgh where you showed us the caricature of you done by the young lad. You really are God's gift to cartoonists!

Which brings me on to why I am writing to you. I am an elder in the Rev. Pastor Jack Glass's congregation in Glasgow. We would like you to address our annual dinner on the 6th June at 7.00pm at the Copthorne Hotel in George Square.

You may be surprised to learn that the Reverend Glass is a staunch Lib Dem supporter!

Yours for Protestantism
Archie Beatty

PS. Could you bring the cartoon on the 6th, I'm sure it will give Jack a good laugh.

To: Archie Beatty
From: Nisbet D (Doreen) on behalf of Donald Gorrie MSP
Sent: Tues, 15/05/01 10:49
Subject: Sectarianism

Dear Archie

Thank you for the kind invitation to speak to your church's annual dinner on 6 June. Unfortunately I am already committed to election activity that evening – the eve of poll – and would earn a major loss of brownie points if I opted out of it. So, my apologies and best wishes for a successful dinner.

By next year I hope we will have advanced a bit towards reducing violence and harassment based on sectarianism from any quarter.

Yours sincerely
Donald Gorrie MSP

To: Donald Gorrie MSP
From: Archie Beatty
Sent: Wed, 16/05/01 10:01

Dear Donald,

We are obviously extremely disappointed that you will not be able to join us on the 6th. Perhaps we could reschedule? How would 12/07/2001 suit you? It is one of our biggest celebrations.

It has been pointed out to me that I may have misunderstood your initiative on sectarianism. Apparently it is aimed indiscriminately at both Catholic excesses and justified Protestant activities.

You are not seriously planning to ban the singing of 'The Sash' at religious services are you? Will it be illegal to jocularly cry at football matches 'Hang the Pope with an orange rope'? And surely it is an inalienable democratic right to sing at social gatherings 'Hail, Hail, the Pope's in Jail. . .'?

I am told that you were born in India but what school did you go to? To put it bluntly, Donald, are you a protestant? You certainly look like one. Let me know if you will be free on the Twelfth. Drop me a line to say what you are up to with this Sectarian malarkey.

FTP

Yours Etc.
Archie Beatty

101 Boghall St.
Moodiesburn
Glasgow G69 1DS

05/07/02

Dear Mr. Gorrie,

I see from my newspaper that you intend to do something about sectarian attacks and abuse. As a victim of this kind of behaviour I think this is long over due.

I run a small Post Office and am an ardent supporter of Rangers Football Club.

On the few occasions when I have worn my Rangers top (Canniggia No. 7) in the Post Office I have been subject to many rude comments about my sympathies. We are asked to integrate by the Home Secretary but when we do we are slandered and verbally abused by the Neanderthals who live here.

On Saturday on leaving the shop I found that these troglodytes had spray painted my car with the slogan, 'Asinder Ya Orange B____d'.

Mr. Gorrie would you like me to drive the car to the parliament so that you can show the country what is happening on the streets? I will not remove the hate filled graffiti till I hear from you.

Yours Sincerely

Asinder Khan

Donald Gorrie MSP
Regional Member for Central Scotland
St Leonard's House
110/112 Hamilton Rd
Motherwell ML1 3DG

22/7/02

Dear Mr Khan

I refer to your letter of the 5th July inst. I was sorry to learn of the damage done to your car recently. Regardless of the sectarian nature of the damage you would perhaps be able to pursue the matter on a simple 'criminal damage' basis, although you should of course take professional legal advice on that issue. If you want me to write to the police regarding the issue please let me know.

My constituency assistant, Hugh O'Donnell did call on you at home last week but you were not available, should you wish to contact him please do so at my Motherwell office.

I would not wish to cause you further distress by asking you not to remove the graffiti from your car immediately, however if you feel that it would be helpful for someone from my office to see the damage please contact Hugh at the address below and he will be happy to meet with you at a convenient time and place.

My own amendment to the Criminal Justice Bill has now been submitted for consideration by Parliament and I am hopeful that it will receive considerable support from parliamentary colleagues.

Thank you for taking the time to write to me regarding your personal experiences of sectarianism. If I can be of assistance in the future please contact me.

Yours sincerely

Donald Gorrie MSP

101 Boghall St
Moodiesburn
Glasgow G69 1DS

26th July 2002

Donald Gorrie MSP
St. Leonard's House
110/112 Hamilton Rd.
Motherwell ML1 3DG

Dear Mr. Gorrie,

I am in receipt of your very kind letter of the 22 inst. I would indeed be most grateful if you would write to the police on my behalf.

Perhaps you could furnish them with my original letter and I would again be most grateful if you could let me have a copy of the letter you send to the Police.

Yours Sincerely

Asinder Khan

Superintendent E Mackenzie
N Division
Strathclyde Police Service
Cumbernauld G67 3 NQ

9/8/02

Dear Superintendent Mackenzie,

I have recently been contacted by Mr Asinder Khan of 101 Boghall St, Moodiesburn with regard to an alleged sectarian incident that occurred outside his place of business.

I enclose for your information a copy of his initial letter to me and his subsequent requesting that I draw the matter to your attention.

You will see from his letter that this incident appears to be the latest of a number of related assaults.

I would be grateful if you could arrange for someone from your staff to investigate these events and perhaps you would be kind enough to advise me of any progress. I am given to understand that no formal complaint has been made by Mr Khan in relation to the incidents.

I am particularly concerned that had the alleged assaults been of a specifically racial nature there is specific legislation that applies, but, given that the basis seems to have been sectarian, there is currently no provision in Scots Law that deals with that.

I would be also interested to know whether you can cite on a generic basis any similar instances within N Division and whether you would view the addition of a clause to Scots Law addressing sectarian crimes as a positive step.

I look forward to hearing from you in due course, and would welcome an early opportunity to meet with you to discuss general policing issues within the Division.

Yours sincerely,
Donald Gorrie MSP

101 Boghall St.
Moodiesburn
Glasgow G69 1DS

12 Aug. 2002

Donald Gorrie MSP
Regional Member for Central Scotland
The Scottish Parliament
Edinburgh EH99 1SP

Dear Donald,

I have had a most unpleasant visit from two members of N Division, Strathclyde Police which, fortunately, I had the foresight to register on my tape-recorder.

As I was recounting my story the policewoman suddenly took exception to me referring to the local populace as 'Fenian nut-jobs'. She also instructed me to remove the poster in the Post Office window of the Pope wearing a Rangers away top. She claimed it was inflammatory and an incitement to a breach of the peace!

As they left the shop the following exchange can distinctly be heard on my tape:–

Policewoman: 'Flippin' Hun.'

Policeman: 'Aye. . . wee blue-nosed bampot.'

Not only did they insult me but they made some fairly disparaging comments about you Donald.

Would you like me to send you a copy of the tape?

Yours Sincerely,

Asinder Khan

P.S. The two constables involved were DC O'Docherty and DC O'Flaherty.

101 Boghall St.
Moodiesburn
Glasgow G69 1DS

27 Aug 02

Donald Gorrie MSP
Scottish Parliament
Edinburgh EH99 1SP

Dear Donald,

As you know the constabulary returned and, at Lib Dem
insistence, charged me with 'wasting police time'. It was all a
bit surreal. When I asked what punishment I could expect for
my heinous and despicable crime the Sergeant said in all his
long experience the procurator fiscal never proceeds with these
cases. A prima facie example of further wasting police time I
think you will agree!

The problem seems to have been that the constables couldn't
make the Superintendent understand that it was all a spoof.
During numerous meetings the poor man just couldn't get his
head round it. I know what you are thinking viz. Crikey! . . .
the police are even thicker than MSPs!!

By the way, Donald, it was a bit rum telling 'The Record' that I
was a 'pain in the backside'. I didn't tell them you were 'a
middle class twit who knows about as much about working
class sectarianism as I know about astrophysics and that you
only want to get your name in the papers to get re-elected'.

Donald, for obvious reasons I would prefer if you didn't pass
this letter to N Division of Strathclyde police.

Yours Sincerely

Asinder Khan

101 Boghall St.
Moodiesburn
Glasgow G69 1DS

15 Aug 02

Christine Grahame MSP
The Scottish Parliament
Edinburgh EH99 1SP

Dear Christine,

As a new party member I attended my third branch meeting last night. The conversation turned to MSPs' pay and I was astonished at the cynicism of our people.

They told me that although a handful had voted against the recent 13% wage rise for MSPs, nevertheless, every single one of the 129 MSPs had promptly pocketed the extra £5,700 (on top of the manifestly generous £45,000) when it was paid.

There was much guffawing when it was pointed out that effectively MPs and MSPs were job-sharing but instead of getting half the money for half a job they in fact get double the money for half a job! 'Then two years later they have the nerve, the gall, the sheer brass neck to demand a 13% pay rise.' More puerile laughter.

A young woman said, 'It doesn't look good to the public.' Then the bombshell. 'Now we have Christine Grahame boasting to the Sunday Times about buying sports cars and driving them all over the south of Scotland, really rubbing the lieges' noses in it!'

I am flabbergasted at this phlegmatic attitude to the universal perception of gold-digging by our parliamentarians.

Christine, as a neophyte to political life I was unable to confound these assertions. Could I ask you how you, as an experienced politician, would have answered their perfervid claims?

Yours Sincerely
Rupert Clubbs

The Scottish Parliament
Ms Christine Grahame, MSP

25th August 2002

Dear Mr Clubbs,

I refer to your letter to me of the 15th, which I have now had the opportunity to read, and before I respond more fully, can I first welcome you to this great movement of which I have been a member for some 30 years.

However I am most concerned at the tenor of the branch meeting, so concerned that I intend to write, subject to your response, to the Constituency convenor. Instead of attacking the enemy, i.e. all unionists, it appears that MSPs have become the butt of uninformed malicious criticism. But let me speak for myself, from a background of 30 years campaigning, selling toffee and tablet to help branch funds, standing as a Council, Westminster, European and Scottish parliament candidate, not to say Elected Member of the NEC and Elected member of Council.

First on the issue of the pay-rise, which I indeed voted for or the money would have stayed with the Chancellor. I thought it was well publicised that I was establishing a charity account for Borders charities with my pay rise under the Westminster 'Give As You Earn Scheme'. In that way the net amount is grossed up and 10% added by the Chancellor. The local Lib/Dems have maligned me as 'buying votes'. Rubbish of course but I can't win either way. However the last thing I need when I am using all my energies to winning Tweeddale is back-stabbing from my own.

Secondly there are the comments about the work-load. How did the commentator come by his/her assessment? My colleagues here work flat out dealing with mail both paper and electronic and dealing with constituency issues, for most of us across at least three constituencies. The remarks should be directed towards Westminster where MPs must be twiddling their thumbs and earning more. What of the volume of committee work, particularly for convenors such as myself? These comments come out of ignorance and malice.

As for the petty remarks about my car, it is so sad to have to deal with so-called colleagues in this response. I never 'boasted' to the Sunday Times. Indeed I never spoke to any paper about the car. Note 'the car', singular. Incidentally it is a second hand Mazda MX5 which cost approximately the same as a brand new Ford Ka. The remark was offensive and spiteful. So you see Rupert, I am asking myself what is behind those comments. For three years I have worked sincerely as I have for decades for Independence. The maker(s) of those comments must be challenged as to his or her motives in endeavouring to undermine my political integrity.

Finally, please feel free to produce this letter to the branch, or otherwise provide me with contact details and preserving your privacy, I will write directly to the secretary. In the meantime I enclose some copies of my parliamentary report which goes out to 700 plus and has done since I came here. I should be obliged if these could be circulated at the next branch meeting and subject to other commitments I am happy to meet these critics at any time.

Yours for Scotland,

Christine Grahame MSP

Don't Vote for an Idiot, Vote for a Clown

101 Boghall St.
Moodiesburn
Glasgow G69 1DS

27 Aug 02

Ms Christine Grahame MSP
The Scottish Parliament
Edinburgh EH99 1SP

Dear Christine,

I 'produced' your letter to Rosemary the member of my branch who was the 'ringleader' of the cynics. She said, 'Christine is trying to pretend she is giving all of the 5,700 quid to charity!?! If she is I will eat my brown felt hat at the next branch meeting.'

She also claims that when you said, 'MPs must be twiddling their thumbs and earning more' you were essentially accepting that MPs and MSPs are job sharing but getting double the money for half the work.

When I pointed out that you said you, 'never spoke to any paper about the car' Rosemary asked when I had 'come up the Clyde in the Banana boat'.

On the question of 'The Reiver', your Parliamentary report, I have to tell you that there was much hilarity and calls of 'straight in the bin'. They described it as 'tatty, amateurish and buttock-clenchingly embarrassing'.

The atmosphere of derision and defeatism is palpable. They say John Swinney is useless, Roseanna is wacky (they could have a point there) and that our front bench people are brownnoses and sooks. I really don't know if I should continue as a member of the SNP. What do you think, Christine?

Yours Sincerely

Rupert Clubbs

The Scottish Parliament
Ms Christine Grahame, MSP

1st September 2002

Dear Mr Clubbs

I thank you for your letter of the 27th August. Given the reported response to my letter and your own views, I should be obliged if you would provide me with contact details for your branch.
I look forward to hearing from you.

Yours for Scotland,
Christine Grahame MSP

101 Boghall St
Moodiesburn
Glasgow G69 1DS

04 Sep 02

Dear Christine,

I have just had a stand-up, blazing row with Rosemary and other members of our branch. The thought of their gratuitously offensive comments becoming public knowledge has 'violently loosened the bowels'.

They now intend to write to you issuing an apology for comments which they claim were meant jocularly.

Christine, could you clear up one point? In your first letter you mentioned you were 'establishing a charity account for Border's charities with your pay rise under the Westminster 'Give As You Earn Scheme'.' Christine, am I correct in arguing that you have used the whole of the £5,700 pay rise for this charity account?

Pour L'Ecosse
Rupert Clubbs

NO REPLY

101 Boghall St.
Moodiesburn
Glasgow G69 1DS

23 Sep 02

Ms. Rhoda Grant MSP
Scottish Parliament
Edinburgh EH99 1SP

Dear Rhoda,

My thirteen year old daughter now lives on Lewis with her
Father. She has been chosen to represent New Labour in mock
elections at her school.

Both her father and I were quite proud when she was selected
but horrified when we heard what her Modern Studies teacher
said to her.

'Alexandra, as the New Labour candidate, will have the tricky
political task of pretending to be on the left of the spectrum
while building private prisons, privatising schools and
hospitals, part privatising the Post office and Air traffic control,
privatising the housing stock, recklessly privatising the nuclear
industry, in fact acting just like a Tory.'

As you can imagine both my ex-husband and I were
flabbergasted at this deplorable attempt to misguide young
minds against the Labour party. I am, though, at a loss as to
what to do about it.

I wouldn't want the young woman to lose her job over it but I
think something should be said. Rhoda, how should I handle
this?

Yours Sincerely

Roberta (Bobby) Caldwell-Smyth

Ms. Rhoda Grant MSP
Scottish Parliament
Edinburgh EH99 1SP

2 October 2002

Ms Roberta Caldwell-Smyth
101 Boghall St.
Moodiesburn
Glasgow G69 1DS

Dear Roberta

Thank you for your letter.

I can understand your pride when Alexandra was chosen to take part in the mock elections at school. Similarly, I can understand your concern at her teacher's comments.

I would suggest that you, or Alexandra's father, have an informal word with the teacher herself or with the headteacher. This would allow your concerns to be heard but would not take the form of an official complaint against the teacher.

I enclose a mock elections pack for Alexandra and hope this will be of use to her – please let me know how she gets on.

Best wishes.

Yours sincerely

RHODA GRANT, MSP

Don't Vote for an Idiot, Vote for a Clown

From: Rosemary Hannay hannayrosemary@hotmail.com
Sent: Thursday, September 06, 2001 5:02 PM
To: iain.gray.msp@scottish.parliament.uk
Subject: Duncan Hamilton MSP

Hi Iain,

I saw you being interviewed on TV with that ridiculous article Duncan Hamilton the juvenile Nat. You slapped him down comprehensively. What a buffoon he seemed when you asked him what specific proposals the nationalists would oppose and he couldn't produce a single one. Magisterial!

I was discombobulated, however, when he said, 'I love Iain'.

I think you should report him to Lord Steel! I have heard reports that he wears makeup!! He is obviously trying to tar you with the same pink paint brush. I am nearly 80 years of age but I think you should have whiskered him.

Have you seen the vacuous articles he writes for the Evening Times? They are the most fatuous drivel I've ever seen. The boy is a balloon.

Keep up the good work. Drop me a line and tell me you don't fraternise with poltroons like Hamilton and his chubby pal Wilson.

Dr. Rosemary Wilson

From: Iain Gray MSP
To: Rosemary Hannay
Sent: Thurs, 6 Sep 2001 17:23
Subject: RE: Duncan Hamilton

Dear Dr. Wilson,

Thank you for your kind words!

Best wishes

Iain Gray

From: Rosemary Hannay
To: Iain Gray MSP
Sent: Fri, 7 Sep 2001 11:07

Hi Iain,

I noticed that I signed my e-mail to you Rosemary Wilson! I must be going off my head. It should of course have been Rosemary Hannay.

Having reread my letter I suddenly realised that it could have been construed as homophobic. Nothing could be further from the truth. If young Hamilton wants to wear make-up that's his business and if Andrew Wilson chooses to broadcast it all over cyber space that's up to him.

I believe there are a number of openly gay MSPs. Fair enough. OK. Live and let live. I have no idea who they are. Although I have never cared for the cut of Frank McAveety's jib. (You remember when he dyed his puddin' bowl coiffure) All that irrational abrasiveness must be hiding a terribly hurt little boy. Ross Finnie looks as if he might be gay but then he looks like he might be a protestant as well.

Those ears and the tiny facial features point to infantile alcohol syndrome. But hasn't he got a beautiful speaking voice – I am sometimes tempted to believe the nonsense he spouts.

Tom McCabe is another one who strikes me as someone with a closet full of exotic and shameful secrets.

Iain, I will be in Edinburgh next Thursday could I drop into the parliament for a cup of tea and a bun with you? Unless I hear from you that it is inconvenient I'll pop through your door about 09:30.

Dr. Rosemary Hannay

From: Rosemary Hannay [hannayrosemary@hotmail.com
Sent: 01 August 2001 12:54
To: duncan.hamilton.msp@scottish.parliament.uk
Subject: Scotland's Internet deficit

Hi Duncan,

Would you be prepared to come and talk to a class of 15 year olds about the relative backwardness of Scotland in internet utilisation? I saw your article in the Evening Times and my class are doing a project on this very subject.

I am told you are the youngest MSP (and from your photo the best looking) so you will be able to relate to the children without being patronising. We had Mike Russell MSP visit the school on another subject and he was quite unsuitable. A bumptious know-all as I am sure you are well aware.

When your article is boiled down to its absolute essence are you simply saying that the Internet is good or was there a more opaque and subtle point you were trying to impart?

I look forward to hearing from you and we can make a rendezvous for you to visit the school at a mutually convenient time.

Regards

Dr. Rosemary Hannay

Hamilton and the internet deficit

From: duncan.hamilton.msp@scottish.parliament.uk
To: Rosemary Hannay
CC: Kenneth MacColl
Subject: Scotland's Internet Deficit
Sent: Mon, 6 Aug 2001

Rosemary

I would be delighted – if you had a chance to ring the office on 0131 348 5700 or failing that on 01631 571359 if the Parliamentary office is shut. I am away until the end of August on annual leave but I would be very happy to come in whenever it suits.

As for the article, it was about the need for access to the internet, the need to sell that added value from a government and business perspective and really about the paucity of thinking on the area of e-Govt and e-Commerce in this country by comparison with other nations around the globe.

Look forward to hearing from you.

Duncan

From: 'Kenneth MacColl' kenneth@highlandsislands.fsnet.co.uk
To: Rosemary Hannay
Subject: Scotland's Internet Deficit
Sent: Mon 6 Aug 2001

Rosemary,

Duncan has copied me your invitation to speak to class.

I am in his Oban constituency office, the bloke at the end of the 01631 telephone number he quoted to you. I note that he has accepted your invitation but does not know where he might have to visit.

He confidently stated that it would be in the ET circulation area. I suggested it might be on Muckle Flugga. Please advise!

I know that there is plenty time before school/parliament goes back but I have your e-mail address on file.

Ken
Ken MacColl PA

From: Rosemary Hannay
To: 'Kenneth MacColl' kenneth@highlandsislands.fsnet.co.uk
Subject: School visit
Sent: Mon, 6 Aug 2001

Dear Ken,

Thank you for your e-mail. I'm afraid I don't know what the 'ET circulation area comprises' and I am totally ignorant of the whereabouts of 'Muckle Flugga'.

We, that is, 'The College of Islamic Studies', are at Whithorn in Dumfries and Galloway. Duncan should come down the A714 and he will see a large sign for the college on the left just before the town. If he misses it, just ask anyone in town where we are, everyone knows the college!

Any date in August or September will suit us as the girls are all boarders. I have told them we are to receive a beautiful young MSP and they are all very excited at the prospect.

Could you let me know the prospective date asap so that I can make arrangements for Duncan's logement? Does he have any special dietary requirements?

God is Great.
Dr. Rose Hannay

From: Kenneth MacColl
To: Rosemary Hannay
Subject: RE: Internet Deficit
Sent: Wed, 8 Aug 2001

Dear Rosemary,

Thank you for your reply. I note that you have copied this to DH so he will doubtless reply to you in due course.

Sorry for being obtuse. . . The ET circulation area is that area covered by the Evening Times. Muckle Flugga is the northernmost point on the Shetland isles and a long long way from most of Scotland. The parliament resumes work at the start of September but in the recess he usually does constituency work and tries to take a break. God is indeed Great.
Ken

Hamilton and the internet deficit

From: Rosemary Hannay hannayrosemary@hotmail.com
Sent: 02 October 2001 23:13
To: duncan.hamilton@scottish.parliament.uk
Subject: School visit

Hello Duncan,

I have arranged for you to speak to our pupils as agreed next Friday evening 12th Oct. about seven o'clock. If this is in any way difficult for you we could reschedule. If you let me know ASAP I would be most grateful. (The girls are looking forward to meeting you with barely containable excitement.)

Regards
Dr. Rosemary Hannay

From: duncan.hamilton.msp@scottish.parliament.uk
To: Rosemary Hannay
Subject: RE: School visit
Sent: Wed, 3 Oct 2001

Dear Dr Hannay

With apologies I am afraid I will have to decline as I am in Brussels.

When I am scheduled to be in your part of the world I will certainly be in contact to arrange a visit.

Duncan Hamilton

Don't Vote for an Idiot, Vote for a Clown

From: Rosemary Hannay hannayrosemary@hotmail.com
Sent: 03 October 2001 23:36
To: duncan.hamilton.msp@scottish.parliament.uk
Subject: School Visit

Duncan,

What do you mean 'scheduled'. Can I remind you that the first time you wrote to me you said 'I would be delighted' to come to the school. There was no serpentine caveat about scheduling!

I have 125 teenagers who have been told that you have agreed to visit them. What am I to tell them? I hope your evasive, oleaginous behaviour is not informed by any subliminal prejudice.

I need you to give me a date this month when you can fullfill your long term promise to speak to these children. If not I will have no choice but to turn our correspondence over to John Swinney MSP, Lord David Steel MSP and Mr. Bert White Editor of the Dumfries Argus.

Looking forward to meeting you!!

Dr. Rosemary Hannay

From: duncan.hamilton.msp@scottish.parliament.uk
To: Rosemary Hannay
Subject: RE: School visit
Sent: Thurs, 4 Oct 2001

Dear Dr Hannay

I am sorry you have chosen to take offence at my remarks. I can only repeat what I have said in previous messages. I do not represent your area and while I will be happy to address the school at a time when I am in your vicinity, the needs of the area I represent must come first.

Can I also ask that you resist either the personal attacks or threats. They hardly act as an inducement to make an early visit.

Yours
Duncan Hamilton

Hamilton and the internet deficit

From: Rosemary Hannay
To: Duncan Hamilton MSP
Subject: School visit
Sent: Fri, 5 Oct 2001

Duncan,

I contacted STV with our story and the producer, Sarah, told me that Bernard Ponsonby said it was a 'Cracker'. She advised me that you are now on 2 weeks holiday so your refusal to honour your promise is indeed fishy.

Consequently, on the Thursday 25 October Mrs Hussein (headmistress), Mr Islam (Chair of the school Board), myself and 25 of the girls are coming up to the Parliament to seek an explanation. The 'Crossfire' programme has agreed to send a camera crew on our coach to follow and record our peregrinations.

We intend to meet Mr. Swinney to see if he can explain why one minute you 'would be delighted' to visit our school and the next 'my constituents must come first'. (Although, you can waltz off to Brussels, eh?)

Sarah will arrange for us to meet Mr. Rumbles, chair of the standards ctte. to ask why you don't have any.

Then we will be in the visitors gallery to watch First Ministers Questions.

Will you at least be able to spare us 5 minutes of your precious time on that day?

Looking forward to meeting you, you rotter!

Dr. Rosemary Hannay

Don't Vote for an Idiot, Vote for a Clown

From: Archie Beatty [mailto:snash@maxies.fsnet.co.uk]
Sent: Friday, May 11, 2001 3:41 PM
To: Robin.Harper.msp@scottish.parliament.uk
Subject: General Election

Hi Robin,

I caught you on Radio Scotland today with that ignorant article Lesley Riddoch. If she interrupted once she interrupted a hundred times.

I was shocked to learn that we are only standing in 4 constituencies. Are we standing in Baillieston? If not, who the hell do I vote for?

Yours Sincerely
Archie Beatty (75 years of age, 55 years a vegetarian)

From: Harper R (Robin) Robin.Harper.msp@scottish.parliament.uk
Sent: Tues,15/05/01 16:59
To: 'Archie Beatty'
Subject: RE:General Election

Dear Archie

I actually get on very well with Lesley and enjoy going on her show – she's just trying to move things on at a good cracking pace! I'm afraid we're only standing in Glasgow Kelvin, Stirling, Edinburgh Central and Ross, Skye and Inverness West.

I'm afraid I cannot give any advice on who to vote for.

There's so little difference between the other Parties on the environment in terms of their record, that I'm tempted to say forget the Parties and vote for the candidate you think would make the best job.

Best wishes
Robin

From: Archie Beatty [mailto:snash@maxies.fsnet.co.uk]
Sent: Wednesday, May 16, 2001 5:23 PM
To: Harper R (Robin), MSP
Subject: Capital Question

Hello Robin,

Many thanks for your reply. Some Tories canvassed me today at Safeway's. They are very firm on capital punishment and since you report no difference between them and the others I'll probably plump for them. I think most Green supporters will do likewise in Baillieston.

While I have your attention do we (the Greens) have a formal policy on the death penalty? I take it we would support hanging as the most environmentally friendly? Although, if the electric chair was linked to wind turbines I suppose that would be OK. We would definitely be against lethal injections because of the chemicals they release into the environment.

The socialists had a stall in Baillieston High St. When I told them I was a Green but would be voting Tory on your recommendation they became agitated and quite abusive and shouted obscenities at us as my wife and I beat a hasty retreat. Flippin' fanatics.

Drop me a line on where we stand on the rope.
Looking forward to hearing from you.

Yours Etc.
Archie Beatty

From: Harper R (Robin) Robin.Harper.msp@scottish.parliament.uk
Sent: Thurs, 17/05/01 16:01
To: 'Archie Beatty'
Subject: RE: Capital Question

Dear Sir

I have to tell you that the Green Party would never support the re-introduction of hanging or any other form of capital punishment. I have to tell you that our prison policy stresses the possibilities of reform and that prisoners should be treated as human beings and returned to society in better condition than they were when they entered prison.

I most certainly did not recommend you to vote Tory. I said quite clearly that I was not prepared to recommend any of the other parties and I was quite clear that you should simply make up your mind on the basis of which candidate was best.

The Green Party is so firmly against the re-introduction of capital punishment I would have to say to you, if you are a member, that you should seriously consider leaving the Party. I am afraid that your views would certainly not be welcome within our ranks.

Yours sincerely
Robin Harper MSP

From: Archie Beatty
Sent: Thurs, 17/05/01 16:35
To: Robin.Harper.msp@scottish.parliament.uk
Subject: Hemp

Robin,

Keep the heid!! I am bewildered by the splenetic tone you have adopted in your last e-mail.

Are you seriously arguing that it is better to power electric chairs by nuclear energy than wind energy? Do you seriously prefer lethal injections to the rope? (Hemp ropes are a natural material, bio-degradable and thus eco-friendly.) On the continent 'Les Verts' favour Madame Guillotine which being hand powered they consider both safe for the environment and more personal.

I accept that you did not recommend that we vote Tory only that it was a valid option for Greens.

Let's say no more about it. Mrs Beatty and I will be in Edinburgh next Wednesday and we'll pop in to your office at the Parliament for a cup of tea and a 'frank exchange of views' on environmentally responsible methods of judicial execution.

So unless I hear from you that it is inconvenient I'll see you next week.

Yours Etc.
Archie Beatty

From: hannayrosemary@hotmail.com
To: hugh.henry.msp@scottish.parliament.uk
Subject: MSP Biographies
Date: Mon 3 Sep 2001 09:46

Hi Hugh,
I am preparing a book of biographies of all the MSPs for Harper Collins. The book will appear towards Xmas 2001.

Would you kindly confirm two points for us. What is the exact qualification in Accountancy you hold and were you indeed a member of the Militant Tendency in the 80s?
Thanking you in anticipation.
Dr. Rosemary Hannay

From: Paul.Thomson@scottish.parliament.uk
To: hannayrosemary@hotmail.com
Subject: Hugh Henry
Date: Thurs, 6 Sep 2001 13:13

Hugh Henry has a qualification in Bachelor of Accountancy.
Thanks
Paul

From: hannayrosemary@hotmail.com
To: Paul.Thomson@scottish.parliament.uk
Subject: Biographical details
Date: Thurs, 6 Sep 2001 14:15

Hi Paul,
Thank you for your very prompt reply to my request for info. I note that you omitted to say anything on the other delicate issue that I raised. I am fairly sure, from various sources, not least the Militant Newspaper for the 80s, that Hugh was a prominent member of that organisation. However, if Hugh is in any way troubled about that appearing in the forthcoming book I will be happy to excise it.
As we are going to press quite soon I would be grateful if you could let me know his wishes in this regard. (We were all young once)
If I don't hear from you to the contrary I'll include the details of his membership in Militant.

Dr. Rosemary Hannay

From: Paul.Thomson@scottish.parliament.uk
To: hannayrosemary@hotmail.com
Subject: Hugh Henry
Date: Mon, 10 Sep 2001 15:19

Hi Rosemary,
Please find enclosed Hugh's response to your last e-mail

'Dear Dr Hannay
I am unaware of any confirmation in any sources that I was a
member of any organisation. My political activity and my views
however, were well known and never hidden.
I am sure that anything you publish will accurately reflect events.'

Cheers,
Paul

From: hannayrosemary@hotmail.com
To: Paul.Thomson@scottish.parliament.uk
Subject: Militant
Date: Mon, 10 Sep 2001 16:07

Hi Paul,
Does that mean Yes or No?
Regards
Dr. Rosemary Hannay

From: hannayrosemary@hotmail.com
To: Paul.Thomson@scottish.parliament.uk
Subject: Militant
Date: Mon, 17 Sep 2001 11:51

Hi Paul,

Here is a section of the entry for Mr. Henry. If he would like any
additions or anything altered please let me know within 6 days and I
will be happy to comply.

'Hugh Henry is the only New Labour MSP who is openly a
revolutionary Marxist. He was a leading activist in the Poll Tax riots
of the early 90s. He participated in the infamous invasion of
Glasgow's City Chambers when Councillors and staff were verbally
abused and some vandalism occurred. He only narrowly avoided
prison on various occasions and is thought to have the most
extensive dossier of any MSP held by Special Branch.

'His apostasy from Trotskyism was so swift and violent that he is thought to maintain no contacts with his former associates in Militant. He is now universally reviled and despised by his erstwhile comrades. PFI, private prisons, privatisation of Air Traffic Control, bombing Iraq and selling off the housing stock to the banks would once have caused Hugh untold anguish. Now he smiles as he votes with equanimity for Tory policies.

'He is one of the parliament's more indolent MSPs. He rarely speaks in the chamber or appears on TV and is said to consider the 3 day week that MSPs work as excessively onerous. His political past means he has been offered no posts in the Executive and since he is widely distrusted his career has ground to a shuddering halt.

'How did this recent turncoat claw his way, over the heads of time served Labour sycophants, to the parliament in so short a time? Insiders point out that this once principled socialist now has a snout the colour of a Cadbury's Flake.'

As you can see, Paul, the entries are meant to be light-hearted and a little scurrilous. I am sure Hugh has a sense of humour and will enjoy the equally irreverent biographical details of his colleagues!

However, if Hugh is unhappy about anything do not hesitate to let me know.

Regards
Dr. Rosemary Hannay

From: Hugh.Henry.msp@scottish.parliament.uk
To: hannayrosemary@hotmail.com
Subject: RE: Biographical Details
Date: Mon, 17 Sep 2001 15:23

I have deleted your original e-mail, could you please outline again what publication this information is to be printed in.

If you could also give me a contact number in case Hugh wants to get in touch, it would be appreciated.

Cheers

Paul

101 Boghall St.
Moodiesburn G69 1DS

27 Nov 02

Hugh Henry MSP
Anchor House, Blackhall Lane
Paisley PA1 1TA

Dear Hugh,

First congratulations on your elevation to the position of
Deputy Justice Minister. I think we can all agree that your
predecessor, Dr. Richard Simpson, is simply a poltroon with
absolutely no grounding in the Labour movement. He could as
easily have been a Tory.

I write to draw your attention to a poisonous piece by that
reptile Frances Horsburgh writing in this morning's Herald.
Referring to you she says, 'At one time seen as on the factional
left of the Labour Party, Mr Henry had a torrid political time as
leader of Renfrewshire council between 1995 and 1999. So
extraordinary bitter were the political battles between Labour
and the SNP, and sometimes within the Labour group, that
police were often called to the chambers.'

Hugh, the outrageous sub-text here is that you were for many
years a Trotskyite thug! She continues, 'However his demeanour
is hardly pugilistic and has been compared to a successful under-
taker.' You can't help it if you look like a pox doctor's
assistant!?! Then she says, 'he has expressed concerns about
passive smoking and once urged a ban on smoking anywhere.'
This is clearly intended to mean you are some kind of nut job.

Hugh, I take it you will be going to litigation to nip this
insidious campaign in the bud. Here's a fiver. A modest contribution to your costs but I feel a principle is at stake. The cash is
to fight any legal case, mind. I don't want it disappearing into
one of Jack's dodgy 'Red Rose Dinner' type accounts!

Yours for Some Press Honesty
Roberta Caldwell-Smyth

101 Boghall St.
Moodiesburn
Glasgow G69 1DS

24 Oct 02

John Home Robertson MSP
Town House, High Street
Dunbar EH42 1ER

Dear John,

I met you through the 'Direct aid for Bosnia' campaign some years ago. I saw you on TV, recently, being interviewed in your capacity as head of the new parliament building project. The interviewer demanded what the final cost of the Parliament would be. I squirmed with embarrassment for you when, humiliatingly, you had to admit that no-one had 'a Scooby'. You could only admit 'Approaching 350 million and rising fast. . .'

You have been plunged into a Hellish nightmare by your colleagues. When it became clear that the Holyrood project was going horribly pear-shaped they needed a simple soul of impeccable honesty to bamboozle the gullible populace. They have now squandered your reputation for probity and rectitude by making you the dissembling mouthpiece for an indefensibly profligate misuse of public money.

As reported in 'All the First Minister's Men' the Scottish Office initially tried to hoodwink the electorate by claiming that a building could be built for as little as £10 million. The present cost is the biggest overrun in a building project in history (over 300%).

Get out of it John! If you care anything about what history will say about you, let some other poltroon carry the can for this financial lunacy, criminal waste and the inevitable debacle when the truth is finally dragged into the daylight.

However, I know a Captain of your integrity is unlikely to take to the lifeboats as the shipwreck goes down, so here's a fiver to help you with the cost of the Parliament. (No slipping it into Labour Party funds, mind). If a room in the new building could be named after me I would be prepared to make a generous contribution to your 'election expenses' John.

Yours Sincerely, Roberta Caldwell-Smyth

John Home Robertson MSP (East Lothian)
Constituency Office
The Town House, High Street
Dunbar EH42 1 ER

28th October 2002

Ms Roberta Caldwell-Smyth
101 Boghall St.
Moodiesburn
Glasgow G69 1DS

Dear Ms Caldwell-Smyth

Thank you for your letter of the 24th October. I welcome your interest in Scotland's new parliament building at Holyrood although I am obviously disappointed at the negative perception of the Holyrood Project that has been generated by negative reporting in the media.

I took responsibility as Convenor of the Holyrood Progress Group a year ago, long after decisions were made about the site, the architect and the type of contract that had been adopted. However I am convinced that Donald Dewar and his colleagues were right to select a site in the historic centre of our capital city and to appoint a world renowned architect to design a fine building that will be a symbol of a confident new Scotland as well as a working home for our new democracy. And I am satisfied that alternative arrangements for the design and construction of the building would have taken longer and cost more.

The figure of £40 million which is regularly cited in the press as the initial cost estimate is in fact completely irrelevant. That could only have provided for a basic utilitarian building on an out of town site with a comparatively short life span. The building that is now being constructed was always going to cost in the region of £200 million and I am obviously disappointed that factors completely beyond our control have led to further escalation. The project team has been striving throughout to contain costs without compromising quality. However, factors such as the boom in the building industry in the Edinburgh area and increased attention to the risk of terrorist attacks have added to cost problems.

I take some comfort from the fact that many other buildings that are now regarded as international architectural icons (such as the Houses of Parliament in London and the Sydney Opera House) have experienced similar criticisms and cost problems. I am confident that the Holyrood building will be accepted as a tremendous national asset when it is completed next year and I am certainly not going to lose my nerve at this stage!

I am still involved in Edinburgh Direct Aid, indeed I hope to take part in a delivery of aid to Bethlehem around Christmas with EDA, and so can I suggest that that might be a more appropriate place for you to send your £5.

Yours sincerely

John Home Robertson
MSP for East Lothian

101 Boghall St.
Moodiesburn
Glasgow G69 1DS

20 Nov 02

John Home Robertson MSP
Town House, High St.
Dunbar EH42 1ER

Dear John,

Many thanks for the return of my fiver. I opened my 'Scotsman' the other day to the headline, HOLYROOD COSTS HEADING FOR £400,000,000. I did warn you John.

Yesterday, I cringed as Sir David tried to defend the new building costs on 'Newsnight'. It was the most, nauseating, toe-curling, ignominious pantomime I had ever clapped eyes on in all my 72 years. That is, it was, until I saw you being torn to pieces today on TV.

John, I hope someone taped the interview for you? Have you any idea how moronic you appeared when asked if you could tell us how much the final cost would be and you pathetically whispered, 'No'. Then asked if you could tell us when it would be finished you murmured, 'No'.

John, the shambles of the new building is not your responsibility. It was Donald's folly. If he was alive today his reputation would be in tatters. Instead it is you who is forced to stand in front of the whole Scottish nation and proclaim yourself the biggest numpty for 300 years. Abandon ship now John!! Do you really want historians in 300 years time to be writing, 'John Home Robertson MSP is the biggest idiot Scotland has ever produced'?

I will be in Edinburgh next Thursday, 28th Nov with my husband. We will visit your office to finalise, as previously discussed, my donation to your election fund. Unless I hear from you that this is inconvenient I will pop through your door at 09:30. Is a cup of tea and a chocolate biscuit out of the question?

Yours Ever
Roberta Caldwell-Smyth

PS. We recently discovered (to our astonishment) from the press, that you are something of a millionaire. 30 million according to my newspaper. My husband said, jocularly, that on the telly you 'look like a pox doctor's assistant'. Lash out on a respectable looking suit for God's sake man!!

John Home Robertson MSP (East Lothian)
Constituency Office
The Town House, High Street
Dunbar EH42 1 ER

25th November 2002

Mrs R Caldwell-Smyth
101 Boghall St
Moodiesburn
Glasgow G69 1DS

Dear Mrs Caldwell-Smyth

Thank you for your further letter – I hope that it makes you feel better to pen such missives.

I will simply say that it is a great a mistake to believe everything that you read in the press, and that I am confident that Scotland's new Parliament building is going to be as big an asset for Scotland as the Sydney Opera House is for Australia. I am certainly not going to abdicate my responsibility to see this project through to a successful completion.

Yours sincerely
John Home Robertson MSP for East Lothian

From: Rosemary Hannay
To: gordon.jackson.msp@scottish.parliament.uk
Subject: Political Slander
Sent: Thurs, 2 Oct 2001

Hello Gordon,

I have just obtained, from Riddrie Library, a copy of 'Scotland Reclaimed' by that notorious separatist Murray Ritchie. I am apoplectic with outrage!!

In it he makes the most outrageous claims of impropriety in your selection process in Govan. Gordon, have you seen these slurs on your character? Have you considered suing The Herald and this poltroon of a political editor? He claims 'all sorts of ghastly and blatant malpractice' went on. 'Gordon is. . . plainly embarrassed.' (Page 37) Gordon, can he get away with this mendacious fiction?

Juxtaposed with the lurid details of the Sarwar trial ('. . . the party will want to know why he lied about the famous loan – which the Crown said was a bribe – to one of his rival candidates, Badar Islam' and 'the bag full of twenty pound notes') a torrid atmosphere of sleaze and corruption in Govan is intentionally invoked.

I intend to put a motion to my constituency party and to my branch of Unison, utterly condemning these egregious lies and slanders. I will write to Ritchie and his editor to record my disgust with his 'bitch' journalism.

Gordon, what else should I do?

Fizzing
Dr. Rosemary Hannay

From: Mary.Austin@scottish.parliament.uk
To: Rosemary Hannay
Subject: Political Slander
Sent: Fri, 12 Oct 2001

Please see attached response from Mr. Jackson,

MARY F. AUSTIN P.A. to GORDON JACKSON MSP

GORDON JACKSON MSP
GLASGOW GOVAN CONSTITUENCY
Constituency Office: 247 Paisley Road West
Glasgow, G51 1NE
PHONE: 0141 427 7047
FAX: 0141 427 9374

Our Ref: WGJ/MFA/M

12th October, 2001

E-mail communication to Rosemary Hannay

Thank you for your E-mail. I think that the one thing I have learned about being a politician is that a fairly thick skin is more or less essential.

I think the book was written a couple of years ago so at this state I would be inclined to ignore it but many thanks for pointing out what was written.

Yours sincerely,
GORDON JACKSON MSP

From: hannayrosemary
To: mailto:gordon.jackson@scottish.parliament.uk
Subject: Political Slander
Sent: Sun, 14 Oct 2001

Hi Gordon,

Thanks for your e-mail of the 12th October. I must say I am thunderstruck at your equanimity in the face of these most scurrilous allegations. The book was only published in 2000.

Have you seen it? Are you really nonchalant about Ritchie claiming that you were '. . . put there under Sarwar's influence'? (Page 36) Do you intend to meekly accept his claims that 'One "member" was seen filling in five ballot papers while others, who spoke no English and had never been seen at Labour meetings before, were only able to say the word "Jackson" when asked questions'? (Page 37)

Any innocent reader can only form the view that the Govan Labour Party is a sewer of corruption and graft and that you personally must be some kind of bent sleazebag. I feel most strongly that you have to publicly denounce the Herald's Political Editor as a poisonous fantasist. If you don't it is hard to see how you can avoid people drawing the conclusion that in some respects Murray Ritchie's version is largely veracious.

I am putting my motion to our constituency party a week on Thursday. Can I say that you consider Murray Ritchie's claims are complete lies and none of what he says ever took place?

Still Fizzing
Dr. Rosemary Hannay

101 Boghall St.
Moodiesburn
Glasgow G69 1DS

24 Nov 02

Gordon Jackson QC MSP
247 Paisley Road West
Glasgow G51 1NE

Dear Gordon,

I see you are deeply involved with another complex and time consuming case in your capacity as one of Scotland's most eminent QCs.

What the cynics, who complain about 'part time' MSPs, fail to understand is that uniquely talented parliamentarians can bring their specialised experiences of real life to bear in the chamber. (Thank goodness your consummate skills were able to persuade the parliament to cap 'Donald's Dome' at £190 million or Christ alone knows where we would be by now.)

I am sure you would agree with me that the duties of a back bench MSP, compared with those of a first class advocate, are not especially onerous. Many Tories and a few of the Lib Dems are full time millionaire farmers and are still relatively competent members of the house. Wendy Alexander has just taken up a post of University Lecturer in parallel with her duties as an MSP. Boris Johnston MP manages to edit our foremost political journal, hold down a TV career and humorously represent the good people of Henley.

It is patently obvious that your public service has grievously diminished your potential earnings. In previous years you earned quarter of a million pounds. Now, apparently, you are reduced to a hundred thousand pounds and your meagre parliamentary allowance of £50,000.

Here's a fiver.

I feel so strongly that Scotland must retain your unparalleled expertise that I am compelled to make this modest contribution. (It's for you personally, mind, I don't want it disappearing into some questionable 'Red Rose Dinner' type account).

Yours Sincerely

Roberta Caldwell-Smyth

101 Boghall St.
Moodiesburn
Glasgow G69 1DS

4 Sep 02

Major Eric Joyce MP
John Smith House
145 West Regent Street
Glasgow G2 4RE

Dear Eric,

You will certainly be aware of the infamous attack on you by the Daily Record's political editor Paul Sinclair in today's paper.

He claims 'Months ago he [yourself] told fellow MPs he was going to apologise to a colleague of mine [Sinclair] he invited to "take outside" with the warning: "I have climbed Mount Everest and I have killed with my bare hands".'

This scandalous assault on the reputation of a sitting Labour member cannot be allowed to go unchallenged. The public probity of a parliamentarian is jealously guarded. If this disgraceful slur is allowed to stand, untold damage will be done to you personally and the party in general.

As a result I have resolved to begin picketing the Daily Record offices in Anderston from Thursday 12th Sep. when Sinclair's next column appears. I have this morning fabricated, in huge red and black letters, a banner which declares, 'ERIC JOYCE MP IS NO THUG'.

I will continue my picket indefinitely until an apology is issued. I will of course contact the BBC and ITV and the rival tabloids. Eric, it occurs to me, however, that litigation may be in the pipeline. If so, or for any other reason, you would prefer me to delay or cancel my protest just let me know. If I don't hear from you I'll be out front of the Record next Wednesday!

Yours Sincerely
Rupert Clubbs

Major Eric Joyce MP
John Smith House
145 West Regent Street
Glasgow G2 4RE

10th September 2000

Dear Mr Clubbs

Firstly, let me apologise for the delay in responding to your letter dated 4th September but I have only received the letter after it was re-routed to me from the Scottish Labour Party at John Smith House in Glasgow.

Let me thank you for the sentiment contained within your letter and the public display of support you have said you would be willing to show for me. It is nice to be reminded from time to time that there are members of the public like yourself who are willing to take such action and make such sacrifices for others.

While I would not wish to comment on the specifics of any relationship between myself and any of the journalists at the Daily Record, you can be assured that I am dealing with the matter in the appropriate manner. In addition, while I would not wish to suggest to you that you should delay or cancel the protest as outlined in your letter, I can see no benefit arising from it at this point.

Once again, let me thank you for your kind sentiments and support.

Best Wishes

Yours sincerely
Eric Joyce MP

101 Boghall St.
Moodiesburn
Glasgow G69 1DS

12 Sep 02

Eric Joyce MP
Parliamentary Office
First Floor 2 Lint Riggs
Falkirk

Dear Eric,

Unfortunately, your letter arrived too late and I had already launched my protest outside the Record offices on Wednesday morning.

The security staff were bamboozled by my banner and at first fairly benign in their attitude. Eventually someone from the editorial staff arrived and she was extremely rude. She said you were a well known 'fantasist' and had served in the army's Educational Corp so if you had killed anyone with your bare hands 'it must have been one of his 'O' level students'.

She also implied you were no alpinist and had probably 'never even been up a set of step ladders'.

The security people then became very abusive calling me a 'nutter' and demanding that I 'F— Off'. They began to push and manhandle me and to cut a long story short I assaulted one with the wooden pole from my banner (which they had torn down). I am not proud of my behaviour as I already have police charges pending.

The constabulary arrived and I have been charged with breach of the peace. I intend to vigorously defend myself and hope you will agree to appear in my defence.

Eric could you drop me a line to say if you would be willing to come to my aid as I came to yours?

Yours Sincerely
Rupert Clubbs

NO REPLY

101 Boghall St.
Moodiesburn
Glasgow G69 1DS

19/04/02

Dear Helen,

As a long time admirer of your robust asperity, not to say
bluntness, I was saddened to see you flounder under the
imperious probing of Mr. Dimbleby on last night's 'Question
Time'. I accept that you were ambushed by his query as to your
attitude to republicanism but to claim as you did that you had
never thought about the question was, frankly, absurd.

My daughter, Chitra (a Lib Dem supporter), howled with
laughter at your discomfiture. 'She's better than Henry McLeish
claiming he didn't know how much rent he had pocketed.'

As a lifelong Labour supporter I was shamed by your
unprincipled squirming. To see a devout Catholic and Labour
politician (especially from Lanarkshire) openly dissemble on
national TV and expect us to believe she had never considered
the future of the Monarchy was disgraceful.

You said you would need two days to consider the subject. Can I
ask you what your 'considered' opinion now is?

Yours Sincerely
Asinder Khan

RT. HON. HELEN LIDDELL MP

Asinder Khan
101 Boghall St.
Moodiesburn
Glasgow G67 1DS

30 April 2002

Dear Asinder

Thank you for your letter of 19 April 2002.

I am a Privy Councillor. I swear an oath of allegiance to the Queen.

I can say with all honesty that no constituent has ever raised the subject with me.

There are no plans or proposals to change the Monarchy, hence I regard the debate as pointless.

Frankly, poverty and the fight to create a modern National Health Service take up more of my time.

Yours sincerely
Rt Hon Helen Liddell MP

101 Boghall St.
Moodiesburn
Glasgow G69 1DS

13/05/02

Dear Helen,

I thank you for the prompt reply to my letter. I have framed your letter and put it up in my post office. It has occasioned much comment from my customers.

However, we are still mystified as to your position on the future of the Monarchy. I accept that your position as a Privy Councillor presents you with a delicate dilemma. But does it really preclude you saying if you personally would advocate a republic like the USA or prefer a mediaeval dynastic, oligarchy like Saudi Arabia or the UK?

I understand that I am not a constituent but as a citizen of Scotland I thought it might be acceptable to pose a question to the Scottish Secretary.

I hope you can tell my customers and I where you stand on this interesting (and on the sub-continent, important) political controversy.

Yours Sincerely
Asinder Khan

Lord James and 'a little crumpled'

101 Boghall St.
Moodiesburn
Glasgow G69 1DS

23rd Jul 2002

Lord James Douglas Hamilton MSP
The Scottish Parliament

Dear Lord James,

I have been reading the paperback edition of 'Breaking the Code' by Gyles Brandreth (a birthday gift from my good lady wife) a former conservative MP and I am flabbergasted at the temerity of the man!

On page 171 he claims, 'I've just been for supper with Lord James. I love him. . . tall, slim, a little crumpled, slightly bent, blue-blooded, sandy-haired, sweet-natured, and can't be as bumbly and daffy as he pretends to be. Can he?'

On page 172 he continues, 'His ministerial car drove us up to St James's and dropped us at the corner. All the way, James told me how much he liked Pratt's. "My favourite club, my father was a member." We got to the street, got out of the car, and James stood there, looking quite lost. "Now where is it? I know it's along here somewhere. Let me see." Like the white rabbit searching for his gloves, he scurried up and down the street until he eventually hit upon the right one.'

The bounder is obviously trying to portray you as some kind of upper class, chinless, nitwit. If this scurrilous attack was from some bolshie I could understand it. But this fool is an ex-member of parliament and a Tory to boot. 'A little crumpled'! I'll give him 'a little crumpled' if I get my hands on him!! Lord James, I intend to fire off a coruscating letter of complaint to Mr Brandreth via his publisher Orion books. I would hate to go off half cocked if you have some sort of understanding with the woolly jumpered twit. Could you drop me a line if you'd rather I didn't complain?

Yours Sincerely, Major Archibald Beatty (Rtd)

25/7/2002

Dear Archie

Many thanks for your letter of the 23rd July. Gyles Brandreth is in my view not a serious source, and is clearly somewhat cheeky.

For my own part I intend to give his writings a big dose of no notice.

With best wishes

Yours Truly
James Douglas-Hamilton

From: Rosemary Hannay
To: Kenny MacAskill MSP
Subject: Chunghwa
Sent: Fri, 10 Aug 2001

Kenny,

Have just read your comments in the Herald on the Chunghwa fiasco. Well done. Your sober, probing and incisive questioning of the Exec. is just what the Party needs to keep its profile raised during the dead time of the summer.

This is in stark contrast to the activities of that ego-maniac Dorothy-Grace Elder. Did you see her letter in yesterday's Herald and the photo of her the day before clashing with mounted Police Officers in the street outside Govanhill Pool? Can nothing be done about this perambulent vexation to the Party? I don't think describing the police horses as racist scum helps the situation, no matter the facts.

You say 'we must change our investment strategy'. Could you explain, briefly, what you mean so I can expatiate at my bridge club.

Dr Rosemary Hannay

PS. How is your Estonia hostelry progressing?

From: MacAskill K (Kenny), MSP
To: Rosemary Hannay
Subject: RE: Chunghwa
Date: Fri, 10 Aug 2001 15:08:43 +0100

Dear Rosemary

Many thanks for the note. The change in strategy comes from Ireland and I think is also accepted by Scottish Enterprise. Basically we should support our own indigenous industry to prosper and grow abroad rather than concentrating on bringing in screwdriver jobs. We must back our own successful businesses and be prepared to take risks. Only that way can we keep the headquarters and research and development. If we don't then we will be in a cycle of competing for assembly jobs with Eastern Europe and elsewhere at the cost of more subsidies and lower wages.

The Irish are seeing the writing on the wall and moving towards trying to support their own folk in a global market rather than bring in others. Hope that clarifies matters.

Re the Govanhill situation I share your concern. There was a rentamob element present who were simply out for trouble. Best to stay out of it. Finally the bar has changed names but still exists. I hope to get over soon to further investigate what I have told my children is their inheritance.

Kenny

MacAskill and the Baltic

From: Rosemary Hannay
Sent: 12 August 2001 23:18
To: Kenny.MacAskill.msp@scottish.parliament.uk
Subject: Economics and Youth

Kenny,

Many thanks for your prompt reply and succinct exposition of our most recent economic thinking. Good to see at least someone has mastered his portfolio.

Last week our Andrew Wilson was quoted in the Herald on the shambles Bear and Amey are making of their contracts for Road maintenance. Our adolescent Economic spokesman said, 'these contracts. . . are proving extremely troublesome'.

Extremely troublesome!!

Boy, that will have Sarah Boyack shakin' in her shoes. For Christ sakes, is this really the best the balloon can do?

Frankly I think he is too callow for the post (and too indolent, from what I hear). Kenny, please put my mind at rest, can we really have confidence in such a pup?

Regards
Dr. Rose Hannay

PS. What Is the new name of your Baltic Bar? I may visit Estonia this Xmas.

Don't Vote for an Idiot, Vote for a Clown

From: MacAskill K (Kenny) MSP
To: Rosemary Hannay
Subject: RE: Economics and Youth
Date: Mon, 13 Aug 2001

Rosemary
Remember it will be Baltic at that time of year. I have been in late
October and November you'll need to wrap up well. Having said
that it's cold but not damp so all is often bright and glistening.
I usually fly to Helsinki in the summer and take the hydrofoil but it
doesn't run in winter though the ferries do. Helsinki is worth a brief
visit if you've never been. The pub is now Cafe Havana. New pubs
open weekly I hear due to growth in tourism.
Re Andrew it's horses for courses. His style is different from mine
but there's room for and a need for both.

Kenny

PS If you need any more Tallinn info happy to oblige or to send
through website details

From: Rosemary Hannay hannayrosemary@hotmail.com
Sent: 14 August 2001 16:14
To: kenny.macaskill.msp@scottish.parliament.uk
Subject: Baltic

Kenny,
I have persuaded the present Mr. Hannay to splash out the dosh
and we are off to Tallinn in December. So I would be most grateful if
you could indeed forward me the details of the website.

Did you see Dorothy-Grace's letter about the riot at Govanhill in
yesterday's Herald. Ye gods! She claimed 'I was dodging round
police horses'. The woman is stone mad. She must be in her 70s as
well.

I note your measured comments on boy Wilson. Unfortunately I
think he is in line to be the next leader of the Party. It is such a pity
that you found yourself in the embrace of a London Bobby at that
Scotland match or you would be the leader in waiting. You are
obviously head and shoulders above the rest. Do you think it is still
held against you?

Rosemary Hannay

From: MacAskill K (Kenny) MSP
To: Rosemary Hannay
Subject: RE: Baltic
Sent: Tues, 14 Aug 2001

Websites
www.tallinn.ee
www.expresshotel.ee

The latter also includes the Olympia as well as others including the Express.

From: Rosemary Hannay hannayrosemary@hotmail.com
Sent: 16 August 2001 10:47
To: kenny.macaskill.msp@scottish.parliament.uk
Subject: tallinn

Hi Kenny,

Many thanks for the Tallinn info. Though, I have to tell you that the present Mr. Hannay has reneged on his promise of an Xmas holiday in the snow. He baulked at the price. Flippin' cheapskate. (He is an ex-Labour Party member so we can't expect any better) I was intrigued by your comment that there were alternatives to Boy Wilson as the future leader.

I've wracked my brain but can't come up with who you are thinking of, unless it is Ms. Sturgeon? Do you really think a chronically irritable budgie with distemper would be a suitable candidate?!? Surely not?

I like Kay Ulrich but she doesn't come across on telly very well. Her voice sounds like her thong has disappeared up her fundament.

None of them come anywhere close to you, or has the same potential. Kenny, put me out of my misery. Who do you think are the alternatives?

Rose

ps Do you see Duncan Hamilton's fatuous articles in Glasgow's Evening Times on Tuesdays? There's a boy who will go far! But methinks not far enough.

From: Kenny MacAskill MSP
To: Rosemary Hannay
Subject: RE: Tallinn
Sent: Thurs, 16 Aug 2001

Rosemary

There are cheap flights available. Either low cost carriers such as Buzz out of Stansted to Helsinki or else try KLM. The best way is to log onto www.travelocity.com that finds the cheapest flights available.

Re leadership a week is a long time in politics and I think that the field is open given that there is not going to be an early vacancy. I also wouldn't be so hard on Nicola. I feel sure she will mellow with age and what she does she does well.

Kenny

From: Kenny MacAskill MSP
To: Rosemary Hannay
Subject: RE: Baltic
Sent: Mon, 20 Aug 2001

Rosemary

Sorry, unlikely to make it at Xmas. I might manage October but even that's problematic. I can get you the name of a hotel in downtown Helsinki at the tram to take for a tour of the city if you want. I have a tartan army pal who lives there.

The hydro foils usually stop in winter but the ferries run. Another Hotel in Tallinn that's worthwhile and cheaper than the Olympia is the Centrall. I can recommend that. It's smarter than the budget one at 5 minutes walk from the old town. Let me know if you need any more info.

Kenny

101 Boghall St.
Moodiesburn
Glasgow G69 1DS

28/06/02

Dear Margo,

As a veteran admirer of your bravura performances in the parliament I pray you will stand as an independent. The party has behaved shamefully. If I can do anything to help your campaign, I will not hesitate.

In 'The Scotsman' diary you publicly denounced your principle tormentor, Kenny MacAskill MSP, as 'that big bastard'. An exact sociological description. High time the rapier of political correctness was abandoned for the verbal bludgeon of plain words.

On the Holyrood programme you said that either John Swinney knew about the disgraceful machinations against you and had therefore sanctioned them. Or, you declared with a ribald snort, 'he is not in control of his office'. No one was left in any doubt that you clearly thought Swinney a four-letter fellow.

Now you are free to tell the truth about the rest of the numpties. If you think Nicola Sturgeon is, in the immortal words of Father Ted, a 'Fekin' eejit' say so. Tell the world that Mike Russell MSP is so full of pomposity and gas it's a wonder they don't have to use cables to keep the balloon on the ground. Kay Ulrich? An adenoidal idiot. Say who the brown noses were. Expose the clypes. Name the scunners!

This is where Dorothy-Grace went wrong. She reputedly allowed Swinney to bully her by telling her to 'f__k!-off' out of his office instead of responding with a colourful Glaswegian retort.

Margo you will replicate the stunning success of Dennis Canavan. Can I be of any help to you?

Yours Sincerely
Asinder Khan

The Scottish Parliament

July 8th 2002

Dear Asinder Khan

Thank you for being in touch. Your support is very much appreciated by all of us in the office.

As yet I am undecided as to the best way to pursue the causes and policies I have supported during my time in Parliament and before. I will be taking time to think about things over the summer.

Yours truly,
Margo MacDonald MSP

From: Rosemary Hannay :annayrosemary@hotmail.com
Sent: 16 August 2001 10:45
To: paul.martin.msp@scottish.parliament.uk
Subject: Sighthill

Dear Paul Martin,

Your article in yesterday's Daily Record was drawn to my attention by a colleague in the staffroom. Can I candidly tell you that I was, for the first time in 27 years, ashamed to be a Labour Party member. (I was subject to not inconsiderable mockery by my fellow educationalists.)

You said 'I care about the residents of Sighthill. . .' and no one will doubt your sincerity. But you go on to say 'The tenants of Sighthill . . . are fed up complaining. . . They shouldn't have to grow tired of asking (for a decent life).'

You will be aware that the residents are living under a Labour UK Government, a Labour Scottish Executive and Labour City Council. They have returned a Labour MP, a Labour MSP and Labour Councillors.

Who exactly are you saying is ignoring their plight?

This gratuitous attack on our party by a serving Parliamentarian is flabbergasting. The UK and Scottish Governments are working in difficult circumstances and doing their best. Your naive carping is entirely unhelpful.

I hope you will honourably admit that you got it wrong and drop me a line to that effect so that I can redeem some dignity in my school.

Disappointedly
Dr. Rosemary Hannay

From: paul.martin.msp@scottish.parliament.uk
To: Rosemary Hannay
Subject: RE: Sighthill
Sent: Thurs, 6 Sep 2001

Dear Dr Hannay,

Thank you for your recent E mail.

So that I can write to you formally I would be grateful if you would provide me with your residential address.

Yours sincerely
Paul Martin MSP

From: Rosemary Hannay hannayrosemary@hotmail.com
Sent: 06 September 2001 22:04
To: paul.martin.msp@scottish.parliament.uk
Subject: Sighthill

Hi Paul,
I live in Riddrie Knowes but if you are too pusillanimous to simply admit you got it wrong on this one, I will drag myself up to your surgery and eyeball you in person. (Is there wheel chair access in St. Phillip's?) All I wanted was a simple e-mail saying that your gratuitous attack on your Labour colleagues in National, Scottish and local government was unconscionable.

I watched First Minister's questions on TV this afternoon and note that they clapped when you asked a question on Sighthill!!

I am utterly bamboozled after the wild attack you made on the party in that shameful rag the Daily Record. (Is it true that your friend Peter Cox, the Editor, has a picture of Hitler on his desk?)

Even at this late date a simple e-mail admitting culpability will suffice.

If not I, with my housebound father and our rheumatic collie Max, will drag ourselves into Glasgow's Beirut, i.e. Ruchazie on the first Monday of next month.

Dr. Rosemary Hannay

From: paul.martin.msp@scottish.parliament.uk
To: Rosemary Hannay
Subject: RE: Sighthill
Sent: Thurs, 20 Sep 2001

Dear Dr Hannay,

Thank you for your recent email concerning Sighthill.
The issues you raise I believe require a full response in writing. I note you live in Riddrie Knowes area however you have not advised me of your address, please advise me of your address so that I can write to you formally. I look forward to hearing from you.

Yours sincerely
Paul Martin MSP

From: Rosemary Hannay hannayrosemary@hotmail.com
Sent: 20 September 2001 19:42
To: paul.martin.msp@scottish.parliament.uk
Subject: Sighthill

Paul,

Your constant attempts to get my address are very unnerving and slightly sinister. Do you intend to come round and 'put the heid' on me? Why do you have to write 'formally'? Why can't you just stick it in an e-mail like a normal person?

Why not just say what you really believe? Which is obviously that the Councillors didn't give a toss about the asylum seekers and only brought them to a totally unsuitable, poverty ridden community and stuck them in vertical slums to blag the government money. That the MPs cynically dispersed them as a deft political manoeuvre knowing the fate which awaited both hosts and guests.

That MSPs may cry crocodile tears but on fifty thousand quid a year (Seventy to a Hundred thousand if they are Ministers) they couldn't give a monkeys about what goes on in Sighthill, Shettleston or any other pigsty where the lumpen-proles are corralled.

That at least would have the merit of honesty and would not be disputed widely. Only don't go about claiming 'you care about the people of Sighthill'. You just sound like a sanctimonious scoundrel!!
Dr. Rose Hannay

Don't Vote for an Idiot, Vote for a Clown

From: paul.martin.msp@scottish.parliament.uk
To: Rosemary Hannay
Subject: RE: Sighthill
Sent: Mon, 1 Oct 2001

Dear Dr Hannay,

I refer to you e-mail dated the 20th September 2001. It is normal practice for me to respond to emails in writing. There are reasons for this.

In your case I intended to attach paper documents to your letter. It would not have been possible to transmit these by email.

Responding to emails in writing assists with my constituency office administration in ensuring that responses are kept on file efficiently.

You suggest that my request for you to provide your address details are 'unnerving and slightly sinister'. I have been an elected member since December 1993. During that period constituents have always been more than happy to provide their contact details so that I could write to them on matters relating to their query. It is normal practice and a procedure I intend to continue following.

Yours sincerely
Paul Martin MSP

101 Boghall St.
Moodiesburn
Glasgow G69 1DS

06 Sep. 02

Tricia Marwick MSP
Scottish Parliament
Edinburgh EH99 1SP

Dear Tricia,

A blazing row has broken out in our branch over MSPs' pay.
Several of our extremely cynical members have been arguing
that, although some MSPs voted against the recent 13% hike,
every single one of them subsequently pocketed the lot.

I remembered that you had been mentioned as one of the
'Magnificent Seven' in the Sunday Mail i.e. one of the 7 MSPs
who said they would vote against the rise. I visited the Mitchell
Library to consult the actual article.

In it you say, 'We didn't ask for it and I am not inclined to
accept it.'

I have argued in our branch that Christine Grahame MSP, for
one, donated all of the £5,700 to local Borders charities and I
have hinted that you did something similar.

Could I ask you Tricia what you decided with regard to the pay
rise?

Yours Sincerely
Rupert Clubbs

The Scottish Parliament
Tricia Marwick, MSP for Mid Scotland and Fife
Scottish Pariament
George IV Bridge
Edinburgh E99 1SP

20th September 2002

Mr R Clubbs
101 Boghall St
Moodiesburn
GLASGOW G69 1DS

Dear Rupert

Thank you for your letter dated 6th September. I voted for
Shona Robison's motion which limited the pay rise to the cost
of living. I said I would not take the increase over and above
that which I voted for.

Since then, I have made three figure donations to Inverkeithing
Highland Games Committee, Fife Miners Heritage Society and
further donations are promised to Fife GM Crops campaigns
and the Maggie's Appeal in Kirkcaldy. I am also purchasing out
of my own salary a new Risograph for use by the Fife
constituencies.

I trust this clarifies my position on the salary increase.

Yours faithfully
Tricia Marwick MSP

101 Boghall St.
Moodiesburn
Glasgow G69 1DS

13 Sep 02

Tricia Marwick MSP
Scottish Parliament
Edinburgh EH99 1SP

Dear Tricia,

Many thanks for your completely frank reply to my letter.

That you are the sole honest member of parliament is amply demonstrated by your willingness to finance the 'Risograph' from your own resources.

Here's a fiver!

Not much, but I know you will use it to help pay for the Risograph and not just stick it in your own 'sky rocket'. (Not a confidence one could have, I think you will agree, with the likes of Roseanna Cunningham MSP or that epitome of pomposity Mike Russell MSP.)

Yours for Scotland
Rupert Clubbs

The Scottish Parliament
Tricia Marwick, MSPfor Mid Scotland and Fife
Scottish Parliament
George IV Bridge
Edinburgh E99 ISP

19th September 2002

Rupert Clubbs, Esq
101 Boghall St
Moodiesburn
GLASGOW G69 1DS

Dear Rupert,

Many thanks for your letter of 13th September. The fiver is gratefully received and will go towards buying ink and masters for the Risograph.

Thanks for the kind gesture. With best wishes.

Yours sincerely

Tricia Marwick MSP

101 Boghall St.
Moodiesburn
Glasgow G69 1DS

20 Sep 02

Tricia Marwick MSP
Scottish Parliament
Edinburgh EH99 1SP

Dear Ms. Marwick,

I fear I have misunderstood your drift with regard to the 'Risograph'. I misconstrued it to be some form of prohibitively expensive medical equipment. I now realise, from your letter of the 19th inst. that it is, in fact, a reprographical device to be used for political purposes by the SNP!

I have recently defected from your party as I was unhappy at the slippery and evasive responses of several MSPs to my enquiries as to what had become of their recent undeserved and extravagant £5,700 pay rise.

In the circumstances I must trouble you to return my five pounds without delay.

Yours Sincerely
Rupert Clubbs

101 Boghall St.
Moodiesburn
Glasgow G69 1DS

10 Oct 02

Tricia Marwick MSP
10 Commercial St.
Markinch
Fife KY7 6DE

Dear Ms. Marwick,

I wrote to you on the 20th of September requesting that you return a sum of money you extracted from me by subterfuge. I have not had the courtesy of a reply.

I had presumed that even an MSP would not stoop to trying to pocket what, compared with your sumptuous salary of £50,000, is a trifling sum.

If you do not restore my money by return of post I will have no choice but to put the matter in the hands of the parliament's Standards Ctte. and contact the press with the story of Scotland's pre-eminent chiselling and money grubbing MSP.

Yours Etc.

Rupert Clubbs

P.S. In your first letter to me you stated, 'I have made three figure donations' to three Charities. Why do you not specify how much? Is it perhaps because it would expose your claim that, 'I would not take the increase over and above what I voted for' as poppycock. If your disgraceful behaviour with regard to my five pounds is anything to go by then the answer is glaringly obvious!!

The Scottish Parliament
Tricia Marwick, MSP for Mid Scotland and Fife
Scottish Parliament
George IV Bridge
Edinburgh EH99 ISP

9th October 2002

Mr R Clubbs
101 Boghall St
Moodiesburn
GLASGOW G69 1DS

Dear Mr Clubbs,

Thank you for your letter of 20th September. I regret the delay
in replying but I am now enclosing £5 which I believe you
donated by mistake.

Yours sincerely
Tricia Marwick MSP

101 Boghall St.
Moodiesburn
Glasgow G69 1DS

16 Oct 02

Tricia Marwick MSP
10 Commercial Street
Markinch
Fife KY7 6DE

Dear Tricia,

Many thanks for the return of my fiver!

I have shown our correspondence to my wife and some of my erstwhile colleagues in the SNP. The universal view appears to be that you must consider me some kind of nutter.

I now see and accept that I have misjudged you and that you are not just trousering the sumptuous wage rise you got from the gullible Scottish electorate.

I hope you will accept my apologies and this five pounds as a symbol of my good will. (The five quid is for you personally mind, not for the party) Have a drink on me and, if you could mention 'Clubbs Wet Fish Shop' in Duke Street as Scotland's finest aquatic emporium on the floor of the parliament, there is more where this came from.

Yours Aye
Rupert Clubbs

The Scottish Parliament
Mr Rupert Clubbs
101 Boghall St
Moodiesburn
GLASGOW G69 1DS

Thursday, 17 October 2002

Dear Mr Clubbs,

Thank you for your most recent letter. I am returning the £5 to you because under the circumstances I could not possibly accept it. I am sure that there is a charity in your local area that is much more deserving of your donation than me.

With best wishes.

Yours sincerely
Tricia Marwick MSP

Don't Vote for an Idiot, Vote for a Clown

From: Rosemary Hannay hannayrosemary@hotmail.com
Sent: 22 August 2001 17:00
To: john.mcallion.msp@scottish.parliament.uk
Subject: Nuclear Power

Dear John,

I have just heard you on Radio Scotland saying that Party policy is that there should be no extension of Nuclear Power and that you expect that to be adhered to by the Government.

John, John, you and I are a couple of dinosaurs! When did party policy last stop Tony and Gordon doing exactly what the CBI wants? I've been a CND activist and Party member for over 20 years and we are now further from socialism and disarmament than ever.

I am on the verge of joining the Lib Dems as I feel I would have more influence on policy (and obviously it would be more left wing).

Can you give me one good reason why that would be wrong?

Dr. Rosemary Hannay

From: John. McAllion.msp
To: hannayrosemary@hotmail.com
Subject: RE: Nuclear Power
Date: Wed, 3 Oct 2001 15:14

Dear Rosemary,

Many apologies for long delay in replying.

I was trying to think of a good reason for you sticking with the party but, as you know, it is difficult.

For my own part, I have decided to speak out and vote for what I have always believed in and to accept whatever consequences follow. If New Labour don't like it, they will have to do something about it. I refuse to be driven out of the party I joined a quarter of a century ago by people who are no more socialist than Ken Clarke or Michael Heseltine.

Yours in comradeship,
John McAllion

From: hannayrosemary@hotmail.com
To: John.McAllion.msp@scottish.parliament.uk
Subject: RE: Nuclear Power
Date: 4 Oct 01

Hello John,

Many thanks for your touching letter. I burn with indignation to see you so isolated and shunned by the New Labour rabble.

John, I hesitated to join the Lib Dems because frankly Jim Wallace always strikes me as being a rubbery combination of Goofy and Mr. Blobby!! Besides, the Libs are just Tories without the low cunning, aren't they?

I had a talk with Big Wilma, another disillusioned comrade in our branch (and like you a Dundonian). She has suggested 'jumping the dyke' and joining the Greens!!

I know you have decided 'on principle' to stay in the Party till they boot you out but when they do would you favour the Greens or the SNP? I like Dorothy-Grace and Margo. They have a bit of fighting spirit (in D-Gs case literally wrestling a Police horse to the ground outside the Govanhill Swimming Pool). On the other hand Andrew Wilson is just a roly-poly monetarist and Duncan Hamilton a vomit inducing moron.

I am a little dubious as Robin Harper always seems a bit dopey to me. If the rest of them are anything like him we'd be more effective joining the Yogic Flyers. What do you think, John?

Hope to hear from you but I understand you may be flat out trying to get expelled!!!

All the Best
Dr. Rosemary Hannay

Don't Vote for an Idiot, Vote for a Clown

From: Archie Beatty [mailto:snash@maxies.fsnet.co.uk]
Sent: 11 May 2001 16:20
To: Frank.McAveety.msp@scottish.parliament.uk
Subject: Lib Dem Lies

Hi Frank,

I am a labour supporter from Tollcross. Those miserable bastards the Lib Dems have just canvassed me at the door. You will not believe what they are saying. There were 2 men and a woman with a red coat who waited in the street.

Even though this election doesn't affect Scotland they asked me if I was happy with my MSP. When I said I was they claimed you were the richest man in Shettleston. I was hopping mad but I didn't know how to counter their lies. How would you have handled them in my place?

Archie Beatty TGWU

From: Frank.McAveety.MSP
To: Archie Beatty
Sent: Tues, 15/05/01 00:18
Subject: RE: Lib Dem Lies

GIVE ME YOUR PHONE NUMBER AND I WILL TALK YOU THROUGH THE TRAUMA YOU HAVE UNDERGONE

TALK TO YOU SOON

From: Archie Beatty
To: Frank McAveety MSP
Sent: Wed, 16/05/01 10:06
Subject: Lying Liberals

Frank,

Thanks for your e-mail. I am not on the phone, in fact I don't have a computer. I come into this Internet cafe in St. Vincent Street before I go on the night shift or for a couple of hours when I come off.

The Lib Dems came back two days after I contacted you and they said they'd come and see me on Friday night. I think the bastards are trying to recruit me. It's worse than the Mormons. The guy is called Ian something and the lassie is called Jo. They are saying that it's not now but when you were a minister that you were the richest bloke in the constituency. I don't know what MSPs get so I couldn't argue the case.

They also are saying the most vicious things about the leadership election when you voted for Henry McLeish against Jack McConnell. So if you could say what went on there I'll be ready for them.

Drop me an e-mail and I'll dazzle them on Friday night.

Yours Etc.
Archie Beatty

PS. I thought we were supposed to be in coalition with these duplicitous bastards?

101 Boghall St.
Moodiesburn
Glasgow G69 1DS

12 Aug. 2002

Jack McConnell MSP
First Minister
The Scottish Parliament
Edinburgh EH99 1SP

Dear First Minister,

Has your attention been drawn to an ignominious report on page 17 of the 'Sunday Times' for July 21 this year?

It claims that 'at the last meeting of the Labour group before the Scottish parliament broke up for the summer holidays. . . (you) praised them (the Labour group) for resisting the urge to brief the press against one another. The irony was not lost on the Labour MSPs. The master of the unattributable back-stabbing comment is, of course, <u>Jack McConnell</u>.' (My emphasis)

'We couldn't stop laughing,' said one MSP.

A mini-tape of the telephone conversation between the Sunday Times journalist and this very MSP has 'serendipitously' come into my possession. Would it be more circumspect to send this item to your office or, as is my own inclination, release it to the press and let events take their course?

Yours Sincerely

Rupert Clubbs

McGugan and the dictatorship scenario

From: hannayrosemary
To: irene.mcgugan.msp@scottish.parliament.uk
Subject: BBC
Date: Monday, 20 Aug 2001

Hi Irene,

As a fellow SNP rugby nut I read your important letter in the Herald today with some interest.

Two points if I may:–

1. You call for 'greater decentralisation throughout the BBC. . . ' but point out that BBC Wales and BBC Northern Ireland are taking a different line on showing the Celtic League rugby from BBC Scotland. Doesn't this negate the essence of you logic?

2. You say 'the Scottish Parliament should have a say in what is aired in Scotland.' Wouldn't that be construed as a little authoritarian and undemocratic and lead to endless repeats of the Holyrood programme? That could prove unpopular as it's the most boring emission in the history of broadcasting as I am sure you are aware. I think we see enough of that partisan wee sook Brian Taylor as it is.

Even Slobodan Milosevic didn't directly intervene to tell Slovenian TV when to show the Rugby. Have I understood your position correctly? (I am a bear of very little brain)

Regards
Dr. Rosemary Hannay

From: McGugan I (Irene), MSP
Sent: Monday, August 20, 2001 10:58 AM
To: Rosemary Hannay
Subject: RE: BBC

Rosemary

Thanks for getting in touch. Your points are valid and well made. Maybe the programme planners in BBC Scotland are a bit less in touch with their audiences or more craven towards their London bosses, who knows? My impression is that in Wales and Northern Ireland, broadcasters do have a wee bit more regard for the culture/

language/traditions of their nations, but I'm sure they wouldn't object to a deal more decentralisation either . . .

With independence, I think/hope we can manage to avoid a dictatorship scenario (!) but I firmly believe that until we have more say over what is broadcast in Scotland, our nation is denied a voice and an identity through the media.

Kind Regards
Irene

From: Rosemary Hannay
To: irene.mcgugan.msp@scottish.parliament.uk
Subject: BBC Bias
Date: Tues, Aug 21 2001

Hi Irene,

Thanks for your very prompt acknowledgement.

Your e-mail provoked violent debate in our staffroom. On the 'Dictatorship Scenario' I said I was much less sanguine than you. I argued that it might be necessary, if the unionist parties resist the democratic will of the Scottish people, to open extra jails and prison camps. Resistance would be met with implacable severity.

Several of my colleagues were derisive and some very hostile. The Modern Studies principal who is a Blairite became incandescent with rage shouting, 'ARE YOU GONNA JAIL ME' repeatedly. Eventually the deputy head had to intervene and the buffoon has been suspended from school.

Which brings me to my point. Irene, would you be willing to come and speak to our upper school on the subject of 'Sport broadcasting and denying a voice and identity to Scotland'? I have cleared it with the Head (who is one of us) and anytime before the end of the year would suit.

Looking forward to hearing from you

Dr. Rose Hannay

PS. The MS principal took juvenile delight in pointing out that Milosevic is a Serbian nationalist and not a Slovenian nationalist!

McGugan and the dictatorship scenario

From: irene.mcgugan.msp@scottish.parliament.uk
To: hannayrosemary@hotmail.com
Subject: RE: BBC Bias
Date: 22 Aug 01

Rosemary

Interesting common room discussions you seem to have. . .

Regarding your suggestion of addressing senior pupils, if the Head Teacher of your school (which one is that?) would like to write to my office with a specific invitation, I will see what can be arranged.

Regards

Irene

Don't Vote for an Idiot, Vote for a Clown

From: Rosemary Hannay
To: angus.mckay.msp@scottish.parliament.uk
Subject: Cannabis
Date: Wed, 31 Oct 01

Hi Angus,

Are you still the Drugs Minister? I met you on one of your fleeting visits to Cranhill. The abrupt decision of that balloon Blunkett to reclassify pot from category B to C has left us Mothers Against Drugs up a certain excrementary tributary without a nautical implement of propulsion.

Gaille McCann is spitting mad. She has been on every Radio and TV news broadcast, raving like a nutter and drowning, as she tries to reconcile the line the government has been punting for years with the exact opposite which is our new line. The poor woman was reduced, on Good Morning Scotland, to ludicrously claiming that category C would lead to more teenage pregnancies!?! (You may have spotted on your visit that Gaille is keen but a 'bear of very little brain')

We now have the situation where all the neds in greater Easterhouse are waving their spliffs at our activists and shouting 'category C' and 'where's your Zero Tolerance noo?'

Can you give me any explanation why this scandalous new policy was sprung on unsuspecting Labour activists out of the blue leading to our utter humiliation in our communities?

Dr. Rosemary Hannay

From: Lily.Kercheran@scottish.parliament.uk
To: hannayrosemary@hotmail.com
Subject: Cannabis
Date: Thurs, 01 Nov 2001

Dear Dr Hannay

Angus has asked me to e-mail you back and let you know that he is no longer Drugs Minister. As Iain Gray is he has passed your e-mail on to him for reply.

Lily Kecheran, Constituency Assistant

NO REPLY

McLetchie and the Removals Agency

From: Archie Beatty [mailto:snash@maxies.fsnet.co.uk]
Sent: 11 May 2001 09:45
To: David.McLetchie.msp@scottish.parliament.uk
Subject: Canvassing in Eastwood

Hi David,
I have just been canvassed in Eastwood by that ignorant article Jim Murphy MP. When I told him I'd been a staunch Tory all of my 75 years he proceeded to try to convince me that New Labour had adopted all of our policies. He said they were pro-NATO and nuclear weapons, pro-business and pro-police. He pointed out that the housing stock transfer was a Tory idea, that the PFIs were all Tory ideas and that private prisons were a Tory idea.

I don't mind telling you that I was rather discombobulated. He argued that a vote for the Conservative party was a wasted vote as they wouldn't win and you could have exactly the same policies from New Labour and back the winner.

I have had a think about this since I returned from the shopping centre and Mrs Beatty agrees with me. We have to go big on bogus asylum seekers. You will be aware that we are swamped by Red Sea pedestrians in this constituency. Send them all back to their own country. That's the only way to have clear blue water between us and the Blairites. Could you drop me a line saying if I'm on the right track?
Yours Faithfully
Mr and Mrs Archie Beatty

From: Menzies A (Ann) on behalf of McLetchie D (David)MSP
To: Archie Beatty
Sent: Fri, 11/05/01 13:22
Subject: RE: Canvassing in Eastwood

Dear Mr and Mrs Beatty
Many thanks for your letter. Always remember when dealing with the Murphys of this world and his New Labour ilk that these policies are ours by conviction – for them they are simply a convenience. We believe but they deceive on these matters. As regards asylum seekers we shall not flinch from our policy of weeding out the bogus applicants a.s.a.p. and deporting them.
Yours sincerely
David McLetchie MSP

Don't Vote for an Idiot, Vote for a Clown

To: Ann.Menzies@scottish.parliament.co.uk
From: Archie Beatty
Sent: Fri, 11/05/01 16:02
Subject: Red Sea Pedestrians

Dear Mr McLetchie,

Many thanks for the prompt reply to my e-mail. We watched you on the TV yesterday and I burned with shame at your discomfiture at the hands of that universally acknowledged thicko McLeish. The fiasco with the advertising vehicle was an own goal. I liked the intervention of D-G Elder 'What's the difference between a Tesco trolley and a Labour Minister? The trolley has a mind of its own!!' Mrs Beatty laughed so hard at one point I thought she had stopped breathing.

We don't mind Dorothy-Grace. She brings a bit of colour to a rather grey assembly. (But doesn't her wig look awfully unnatural on TV?)

I'll come to the point. What you say about the Murphys of this world is spot on. What my wife would like to know is what we are going to do with the Red Sea Pedestrians? They are only bogus asylum seekers who have been here a while? Will we be sending them back?

Will you clear this up for her?

Archie and Sadie Beatty

From: Menzies A(Ann) on behalf of McLetchie D(David)MSP
To: Archie Beatty
Sent: Mon, 14/05/01 16:32
Subject: Red Sea Pedestrians

Dear Mr and Mrs Beatty

Thank you for your letter of 11th May. Last week was not the happiest of Question Times but it shall certainly not deter me from pressing on – sometimes you just have to take your punishment.

As regards asylum seekers already in this country, our policy is to speed up the processing of applications so as to distinguish the bogus from the genuine refugee. We shall establish our new

Removals Agency so that those whose claims for asylum are rejected are quickly deported.

As regards new asylum applicants, as part of our speed up policy we intend that they should be housed in secure reception centres pending a ruling on their case.

Yours sincerely
David McLetchie MSP

From: Archie Beatty
To: David McLetchie MSP
Sent: Sat, 15/05/01 10:02
Subject: Red Sea Footpassengers

Dear Mr McLetchie,

Many thanks for your e-mail today the 14 May. Thank you for making your position on kikes, yids and Red Sea Pedestrians generally absolutely crystal clear.

I am a habitual and regular correspondent with the letters pages of both the Scotsman and the Herald can I quote you on this important subject?

No to making Britain a 'Foreign Land'

Yours Ever
Archie Beatty

101 Boghall St.
Moodiesburn
Glasgow G69 1DS

22 Sep 02

Michael McMahon MSP
Scottish Parliament
Edinburgh EH99 1SP

Dear Michael,

I know you are aware of the unprecedented attack on both the party and you personally in today's 'Sunday Mail'. 'MSPs TAKE HOME MORE THAN £100,000'.

You were singled out as 'the MSP who managed to pocket £114,792 despite representing Hamilton North' (i.e. not some far flung island constituency).

My daughter, Amelia, who is studying politics at Uni adopted the usual myopic attitude that all parliamentarians are money-grubbing, venal numpties up to their armpits in corruption, 'office lets' and fiddling their expenses.

I pointed out that your defence appeared to be simply that, 'I send out a newsletter. . . that is an extra expense. . . '

My daughter claimed, 'almost all but the most indolent MSPs issue newsletters, this guy is obviously recklessly profligate with tax-payers' money'. She was able to produce two examples of newsletters. One, from Christine Grahame (SNP) called 'The Reiver', is a tatty, amateurish and frankly embarrassing effort. An utter waste of public money. The other from our own Elaine Smith MSP is prosaically entitled 'Parliamentary Report'. Again it was a little disappointing and dull.

Michael, I would be most grateful if you could furnish me with a copy of your newsletter so that I may persuade my daughter that her taxes are not being flippantly squandered.

Yours Sincerely
Roberta (Bobby) Caldwell-Smyth

Michael McMahon MSP
Hamilton North & Bellshill Constituency

02 October 2002

Mrs Caldwell-Smyth
101 Boghall St
Moodiesburn
Glasgow G69 1DS

Dear Mrs Caldwell-Smyth

Re: MSP ALLOWANCES

Thank you very much for your letter of 22nd September in respect
of the above issue. I am more than happy to supply you with a copy
of the newsletter I, and my constituency colleague Dr John Reid,
produce for our constituency.

I hope you will appreciate, however, that I do not view the
standard of our newsletter, of itself, to be the most important
aspect of the Sunday Mail article, which you refer to. For that
reason I would like to take the opportunity to proffer a perspective,
which, hopefully, will put the issue within some context and
highlight why this particular piece of journalistic vagary fosters
the very cynicism your daughter exemplifies.

In October of each year the Scottish Parliament Corporate Body
publishes an expenditure report on MSPs' office costs and personal
allowances for the previous financial year. So far it has published
the expense incurred for the financial years 1999/2000 and 2000/
2001. The Sunday Mail combined the reported sums for those two
years to produce a total, which in my case, amounted to £114,000.
This is £50,000 and £64,000 respectively for the two years
concerned.

Although this produces an average of £57,000, quite clearly, there
is a disparity of £14,000 between the two sums. This was caused by
a carry-over of rent and rates bills from one year to the other. The
2000/2001 bill for my office rental includes payments which were
billed in 1999/2000 but not paid out by the Parliament to North
Lanarkshire Council until 2000/2001. The Sunday Mail was told

this. The expenditure report due to be published in October 2002 will show the total allowances for my office in 2001/2002 to be £56,000 which keeps me in line with my previous two year average of £57,000.

The next point of information to be made is that my office rent and rates are very high (£8,500 rent, £2,500 rates) because I chose a main street location in the main part of my constituency. Had I chosen to have an office in a side street on the periphery of my area I could have reduced the cost but been less accessible to my constituents. If I could secure premises in Bellshill with the same visibility and ease of access but at a reduced level of rent I would do so.

As for my newsletter, again the quality is less important than its availability. Dr Reid and I have a joint quarterly circulation of over 3000 copies, which is sent to local libraries, community centres, community and voluntary organisations. We believe that it is important that our constituents know what we are doing and where we can be contacted. It costs almost £1000 annually to advertise my surgeries and contact details in the Bellshill Speaker and Hamilton Advertiser and a similar amount to produce our newsletter. This cost is included in the expenditure report.

That report also includes the salaries of my three staff members (£38,000 total), office telephone and electricity bills, postage, hall rentals for my 48 surgeries/year and any other costs incurred in running a constituency office and carrying out Parliamentary duties.

The combined office and staff costs outlined above amounts to circa £56,000 and is paid directly by the Scottish Parliament to North Lanarkshire Council and those individuals and companies who provide material and services which assist me in doing my job. IT DOES NOT GO INTO MY POCKET! These are costs that are accrued in supporting me in my efforts to serve the people of Hamilton North & Bellshill.

It is appropriate that MSPs' expenses and allowances are published for the electorate to know what is being spent by those they send to the Scottish Parliament. I cannot accept, however, that it is reasonable for the press to misrepresent those figures in order to fill column inches in their papers.

It is only right and proper that the electorate is given the opportunity to elect an alternative next May if they decide that I have not used that money well. That is democracy. In the meantime I will continue to work hard for those constituents and hope that lazy reporting by anonymous journalists in the Sunday Mail will not unfairly influence them against me.

While politicians have a responsibility to conduct themselves properly I believe that the media must share that responsibility and not engender the disillusion so obviously expressed by your daughter.

Again, thank you for taking the time to write to me on this matter.

Yours sincerely
Michael McMahon MSP

101 Boghall St.
Moodiesburn
Glasgow G69 1DS

08 Oct 02

Michael McMahon MSP
188 Main Street
Bellshill ML4 1AE

Dear Michael,

Many thanks for your prompt and very full reply and for the copy of your newsletter.

You admit in your letter that 'the quality is less important than its availability'. I fear I must concur with your faint praise for this 'document'. I am a lecturer at the Glasgow College of Building and Printing and I have rarely clapped eyes on a shabbier or more poorly produced artefact.

To take only one of many examples; a head and shoulder picture of you is reproduced 3 times and each one of them is illegible and unrecognisable. Unless this is intended, so as to hide certain bovine characteristics of the subject, it is inexplicable and deplorable.

Whatever you and Dr. Reid are paying for this abomination (and I notice you avoid the subject in your letter) you are being robbed!

Of course when I showed it to my daughter she merely smiled and sneered, 'So we are expected to believe that two sides of A4 issued quarterly explains why (Michael McMahon) is the most expensive public servant in Western Europe?'

She also pointed out that although you claim that your 'office rent and rates are very high (£8,500 rent, £2,500 rates) we don't know what the average is for MSPs and therefore yours may only be marginally more than normal. If so, then, given that all MSPs pay for constituency offices 'Mr McMahon's extravagant expenditure begins to appear suspiciously prodigal.'

Michael, I must admit that, given the squalid quality of your newsletter and the points made by my daughter about MSPs' rents, I am at a loss to explain why you, a parliamentarian from the central belt, are the most expensive in Scotland.

Michael, do you know what the average cost of office rents is among your colleagues? How much, annually does your 'newsletter' cost and do you know if it is any more expensive than any other newsletters issued by MSPs?

I hope you can clear this up for me so that I can convince my daughter that the whole Holyrood project (£340 million and counting for the building) is not just an enormous and expensive con trick perpetrated on the gullible Scottish people!!

Yours Sincerely
Roberta Caldwell-Smyth

Michael McMahon MSP
188 Main Street
Bellshill ML4 1AE

16 October 2002

Mrs Caldwell-Smyth
101 Boghall St
Moodiesburn
Glasgow G69 1DS

Dear Mrs Caldwell-Smyth

Re: Office Expenses

Thank you for contacting me again in respect of the above issue. I had hoped that my earlier letter had clarified my position on the subject but it would appear that this has not been the case. Indeed, from the contents of your correspondance it seems that I have elicited greater cynicism from you and your daughter than you originally felt.

That being the case I am reluctant to add further to your misconceptions by attempting to reply to the points you make. I fear that no explanation is possible if one starts from the view, which you appear to, that the cost of something is more important than the value of it. Nevertheless, I will attempt to make a few observations in relation to your comments.

First of all, it would appear that I have been unable, in spite of the details provided in my earlier letter, to show that my newsletter was not the cause of my being highlighted in the Sunday Mail. I listed rent, rates, advertising costs, telephone and electricity costs, postage, hall rentals and staff salaries to indicate that the newsletter was far from being the main contributory factor. My mistake appears to have been in not including the cost of publicity leaflets which accompany the newsletter. I have enclosed one of our A5 fliers to indicate the material which we send to all of the groups and individuals who receive the newsletter. The print run for these posters provided me with enough material to distribute for the following three years and amounted to a one-off payment of £800 in the last financial year. The poster also comes in A4 and A3 versions. I hope its quality meets with your approval.

As I pointed out previously the newsletter is distributed to over 300 community groups and voluntary organisations in the constituency and amounts to 12,000 copies per year. My photocopying expenses for last year totalled £185 of which only half was due to the newsletter. I have calculated the production cost of each individual newsletter to be less than 1p.

I would like to reiterate that the quality of the newsletter we produce is secondary to its contents. These contents are aimed at ensuring that as much information on our activities is available to our constituents as possible.

It is not our desire to have the newsletter judged as in a beauty pageant

In relation to the cost of my office in comparison to other MSPs I am afraid that I cannot be of much help to you in assessing the validity of my claim that it makes a considerable difference to my overall costs. I know that it makes my office costs higher than most of my central belt colleagues who I know have either much smaller offices or offices, which are not situated in prominent, high charge locations within their constituencies. Had I chosen less accessible premises I know that I could have reduced my office costs by £6,000 over the two years covered by the Sunday Mail calculations. I preferred to have an office, which cost more but made it easier for people to approach me.

Neither is it possible to compare the cost of a constituency office with that of a list MSP's regional office as the cost for each list MSP is shared dependent upon the number of representatives of each party occupying the office and the staff working there. For example the SNP list members office in Motherwell is the base for their five Central Region members and staff.

Also, as some MSPs base one or more of their support staff in the Parliament Building in Edinburgh it is not possible to compare running costs as any telephone and ICT costs in Parliament Headquarters are met directly by the Parliament and are not recorded against the MSP's office costs. All of my staff members work in my Bellshill office and all of the bills they accrue are charged against my office costs.

I am not aware of having met you personally so I do not know why you felt the need to make tasteless references about me attempting to 'hide certain bovine characteristics'. Equally, I hardly think that a few darkened pictures on a photocopied newsletter can be described as 'inexplicable and deplorable'. What I do know is that I am not 'the most expensive public servant in Western Europe'.

The Sunday Mail column which instigated your correspondence was attempting to portray me as having 'pocketed' the most out of all central belt MSPs. It was that claim and the irresponsible reporting exhibited in that article which I was attempting to clarify. It is unfortunate that you believe that the quality of a photocopied newsletter lends any substance to their report.

In conclusion, while I cannot deny that my office counts amongst the most expensive in the Parliament I believe that my constituents appreciate that I am available when they need me and that they receive a good service.

Yours sincerely
Michael McMahon MSP

101 Boghall St.
Moodiesburn
Glasgow G69 1DS

Michael McMahon MSP
188 Main St.
Bellshill ML4 1AE 24 Oct 02

Dear Michael,

Can I immediately apologise for my 'tasteless' attempt at witticism by implying that you would want to 'hide certain bovine characteristics'. I fully accept that you do not resemble a coo, more like a dyspeptic hippo actually (JOKE).

More seriously, I have been on to the Sunday Mail (so you might be hearing from them again) and they directed me to the MSP allowances statistics on the Parliament's web-site. The figures are pretty damning.

The average cost of an MSP's local office is £9399 although your Labour colleagues Bristow Muldoon and Paul Martin manage to squander the colossal sums of £18039 and £18008 respectively. So you can see that your £13608 cannot explain your being the most reckless profligate in the Parliament.

You have already admitted that your newsletter is an unreadable, clownish piece of tat which costs less than 1p per issue! So the two main reasons you gave to the newspaper for your wild spending do not hold up.

However, the average cost of 'Office Supplies' for MSPs (other than yourself and your Labour colleague Kenneth McIntosh) is £2533 whilst you managed the lavish sum of, wait for it, £12574!!

Michael, are you buying scratch cards and champagne for your staff every week? Are your prolix letters written in gold leaf? Whit in the name of Christ are you spending all this tax payers' money on? Malcolm Chisholm gets by on £810!!

What is the matter with you? If you cannot provide me with a plausible explanation of this dissipate expenditure I will have no alternative but to place our correspondence in the hands of the Standards Committee.

Yours Sincerely

Roberta Caldwell-Smyth

The Scottish Parliament
Michael McMahon MSP
Hamilton North & Bellshill Constituericy

28 October 2002

Mrs Caldwell-Smyth
101 Boghall St
Moodiesburn
Glasgow G69 1DS

Dear Mrs Caldwell-Smyth

RE: OFFICE EXPENSES

I write to acknowledge your recent correspondance dated 24th
October 2002.
I have noted your comments.

Yours sincerely
Michael McMahon MSP

From: Rosemary Hannay hannayrosemary@hotmail.com
Sent: 06 November 2001 22:15
To: pauline.mcneill.msp@scottish.parliament.uk
Subject: Music

Hi Pauline,

I spotted your wee article in 'The Glaswegian' about the cultural discrimination against contemporary music in Scotland. As a teacher of music and a Labour Party member for 20 years I emphatically concur. Your idea to have a representative of Scots music sit on the Scottish Cultural Strategy Focus Group is truly inspired.

One of the 'Proclaimers' twins would certainly deliver the required rocket to our cultural elite. That Mike Russell definitely deserves a kick up the backside. Do you see the effete gibberish he spouts in the Herald every week? The man must be the most pompous narcissist on the planet.

Your quote 'music. . . can be a stabilising influence in lives wrecked by social inclusion' made me smile involuntarily. Pauline, that is why you are a high-profile MSP and I just a chalk face operative. (Are our MSPs trained to get the phrase 'social inclusion' into any situation? Question: Can you construct a sentence combining 'mince' and 'social inclusion' Answer : Mince can be an inexpensive and nourishing repast for families suffering 'social exclusion!)

Pauline did you notice the eejits missed out the last lines of your last paragraph. 'equal footing with Scotland's other' what? Could you let me know how it ends?

Thanking you in advance
Dr. Rosemary Hannay

From: Pauline McNeill MSP
To: Hannay Rosemary
Sent: Wed, 7 Nov 2001 00:59
Subject: Mince

Dear Rosemary

Thank you so much for your email. It was very enjoyable to read.

I take your many points. Yes it looks as though we are trained to always mention social inclusion every opportunity. For me it just describes the class system in a more sophisticated way. I will get someone at my office to get you the last lines of the speech.

The next meeting of our cross party group on contemporary music is 12th December. It is going well.

Regards
Pauline McNeill

101 Boghall St.
Moodiesburn
Glasgow G69 1DS

31 Aug 02

Ms Pauline McNeill MSP
Scottish Parliament
Edinburgh EH99 1SP

Dear Pauline,

I see you have been crossing swords with Tubby Monteith MSP in the 'Evening Times'. You said, 'His jibe (i.e. Tubby's). . . dates back to the days when I was leader of the National Union of Students. . . The principles I fought for then are those I'm fighting for now.' Pauline, why can't those on your wing of the party accept that you have lost the arguments and rally round the New Labour project? Did we fight for PFI when we were students? No, it was a Tory idea as was the 'housing stock transfer' which we now warmly embrace. How about private prisons, did we campaign for them as students? I think not. We are now pro-NATO and pro-nuclear weapons (are you still a member of CND, Pauline?), pro-police and pro-business. We will take money where we can get it, tobacco interests (Ecclestone), arms dealers (Hindduja's) and even gambling interests and pornographers. The student Pauline would be horrified by the policies pursued by the adult Pauline.

After finally ditching clause IV the party we joined no longer exists. We are now clearly on the right wing of European Christian Democracy. This is an honest and honourable place on the political spectrum (and barely distinguishable from the politics of Tubby Monteith who at least has been consistent in his political career) but for you to claim that 'the principles I fought for then are those I'm fighting for now' is both ludicrous and unscrupulous. Don't you think it's time for a little honesty, Pauline? Time to drop the self-delusion perhaps?

Yours Sincerely
Rupert Clubbs

101 Boghall St.
Millerston
Glasgow G33 1DS

27 Aug 02

Bill Miller MEP
PO Box 7212
Glasgow

Dear Bill,

I saw your excellent letter on rates in the Herald last week and remembered that you were a stout 'Friend of the Soviet Union' in your Trade Union days.

You will be aware that 2003 is the hundredth anniversary of the establishment of the Russian Social Democratic Labour Party (RSDLP Bolsheviks). At next year's Mayday celebrations in Glasgow we hope to have a debate on the 'Significance of the Historical split in the Russian Social Democracy'.

Numerous ex-Marxists have agreed to speak including Jimmy Reid, John Reid MP or have indicated an interest: Peter Mandelson MP and Steven Byers MP.

As well as these ex-communists we are keen to have some who were 'fellow-travellers' speak at the meeting. We have invited Tony Benn and one or two others.

Bill, could you give me an indication if this is the kind of event you would be interested in participating in?

'Higher and Higher and Higher
Our emblem the Soviet Star
And every propeller is turning
In defence of the USSR'

Yours Sincerely
Rupert Clubbs
Organising Ctte. for
'Significance of the Historical split
in the Russian Social Democracy'

Don't Vote for an Idiot, Vote for a Clown

From: hannayrosemary@hotmail.com
To: brian.monteith.msp@scottish.parliament.ukk
Subject: Herald Attack
Sent: 21 August 2001 09:52

Dear Brian,

Have you seen Murray Ritchie's monstrous piece in this morning's Herald? He says, 'If Hannibal Lecter lookalike Duncan Smith wins there will be resignations. . . this time among one nation Tories . . . who used to carry huge support before the lunatics took over the asylum.' I take this insult personally as I am sure you do.

He is trying to demonise our wing of the Party. I have fired off a blistering retort to the Herald letters page. Can you do anything from your end?

Dr. Rosemary Hannay

PS. Young Mark Douglas-Home (Herald Editor) will get a piece of my mind the next time I see him!!

From: Brian Monteith MSP.bmsc13972@cableinet.co.uk
To : hannayrosemary@hotmail.com
Subject: RE: Herald Attack
Date: Tues, 21 Aug 2001 10:59

Rosemary,

Well done.
I've tried to look it up on the Herald web site but it doesn't appear to be listed.
I will encourage others to write in too. If that is the best standard that the Herald's Scottish political editor can achieve then the paper really is going downhill.
Can you send me a copy of your letter in case they don't use it.

Brian

From: hannayrosemary@hotmail.com
To: brian.monteith.msp@scottish.parliament.uk
Subject: Lunatic Tories
Date: Tues, 21 Aug 2001 11:52

Brian,
Below is the letter I sent to the Herald.
On a different matter. My husband, an ex-member of the Labour Party recently transferred his old Betamax videos to VHS. During the process he came across exotic footage of an ex-Labour MP (who is now a Nat MSP) at a LPYS fund raising party. Parental guidance is definitely called for in perusing this little video nasty. We will be in Edinburgh next Wednesday and will drop a copy into your office. We would love to meet you if you have 10 mins. So unless I hear from you that it is inconvenient we'll pop through your door about 09:30.
Rosemary

Sir,
Murray Ritchie should know better than to demonise people with learning difficulties by talking about 'lunatics taking over the Asylum' when referring to political parties. A new lexicon is needed if gratuitous offence to families and sufferers is to be avoided.

We in the Conservative party do not object to people who hold strong, or even eccentric views being lampooned in the press. Murray will find, as far as crackpots go, that we Tories are not unique.

Only last week we witnessed the bizarre spectacle of the SNP's Dorothy-Grace Elder wrestling in a Govanhill street with police horses. Eccentric? Or the First Minister openly describing the Northern Ireland Minister John Reid as a 'patronising b——d'. Eccentric? And how about the Presiding Officer's egregious outburst when he described some examples from your profession as 'bitch journalism'! There are wacky characters in all the parties. Margo MacDonald, Donald Gorrie, Lord James Douglas Hamilton, Frank McAveety to mention only the most prominent oddities. Odd, yes, but few would argue completely 'bonkers'.

Is this the knuckle dragging journalism we are to expect from Mark Douglas-Home the new Editor? If so, the Herald, a once great paper will be fit only for lining the bottom of my budgie's cage.

Dr. Rosemary Hannay

101 Boghall St
Moodiesburn G69 1DS

28th Dec. 2001

Dear Bristow,

Has it been brought to your attention that a scurrilous and disgraceful slander against you appeared in the 'Scotland on Sunday' diary last weekend? The author claimed that at the Labour Group's Xmas party, in a private room, upstairs in Deacon Brodie's, you were observed to be 'tired and emotional . . . providing alternative accommodation for [your] supper behind the bar.'

I know you will be outraged, as I am, at this flagrant libel. An MSP's public probity is jealously guarded. It is lamentable that the first time you are mentioned in the Scottish press, since the speculation that you were to relinquish your seat to accommodate Robin Cook MP in his attempt to be First Minister, should be in such insalubrious circumstances.

I knew you when we were on the railways and always found you to be a sober influence and, compared to most BR employees, a relatively moderate imbiber. I, for one, refuse to countenance the idea that you would sully your reputation by such a public display of brutishness.

Consequently, it is my intention to launch a one-man picket of the Scotsman's Barclay House from the 10th of Jan. 2002 (I'll be in Hospital till the 6th). I have already made a large banner which says, 'BRISTOW MULDOON MSP IS NO INEBRIATE'. I will be there every day until we extract a written apology from Alex Massie the journalist involved. I will, of course, contact both the STV and BBC!

Do I have your support on this Bristow?
If you'd rather I didn't, just say so. But I am convinced you will see the justice and necessity in my protest.

Yours Sincerely
Asinder Khan

Newyearfield Farm
Hawk Brae
Ladywell West
Livingston EH54 6TW

4th January 2001

Mr Asinder Khan
101 Boghall St.
Moodiesburn G69 1DS

Dear Mr Khan

Thank you for your letter regarding the diary article in the Scotland on Sunday.

As with many articles that appear in the press, and in particular Diary articles, there is an element of truth and a degree of spin. There is no question, and I would never attempt to deny the fact, that I entered into the festive spirit. It is also the case that my participation in the night's events led to me being somewhat the worse for wear. I, like many other people across the country, partake of alcohol beverage only on an occasional basis, but particularly at Christmas, and I have to say that on this occasion my normal limitations were exceeded.

Whilst my actions on the night are not something to be proud of, I also do not believe that they merit comment in the national press. However, in a society with a free press, newspapers are free to print articles as they see fit. On this occasion I am choosing not to respond.

Can I thank you for your kind words and your offer of support. However, on this occasion I believe that it is best to let the matter rest. I certainly do not intend to pursue the matter with the journalist or newspaper concerned and it would be best if you also let the matter lie. Can I thank you again for you kind words and if I can be of any further assistance please do not hesitate to get in touch.

Yours Sincerely
Bristow Muldoon, MSP for Livingston

Don't Vote for an Idiot, Vote for a Clown

Roberta Caldwell-Smyth
Editor, Church Newsletter
101 Boghall St.
Glasgow G69 1DS

4 Nov. 02

Bristol Muldoon MSP
4 Newyearfield Farm
Hawk Brae, Ladywell West
Livingston EH54 6TW

Dear Mr. Muldoon,

Whilst preparing an article on avarice for our little publication, I stumbled upon the statistics for MSPs' allowances on the Scottish Parliament website. I was astounded to find that whereas the average cost of a local office among your colleagues is £9399 you, Sir, find it necessary to squander the extravagant sum of £18039.

It was not my intention to write to you on this matter but over the intervening period the impression of unrestrained profligacy has grown on me. I mentioned it to the Minister of this parish and several of our Kirk Elders. They were equally astonished that, not content with presiding over the most outrageous overspend on any public building in history and voting themselves an undeserved and egregious 13% pay rise, MSPs are treating themselves to sumptuous, palatial offices.

We have decided that as responsible citizens it is not good enough to simply shrug our shoulders and disappointedly shake our heads. We feel so deeply on this that it is the intention of myself, the Minister and, Mr Eric Bryson (Elder) to visit your Constituency Office on the morning of Friday, 15 Nov. at 09:00 am. to seek an explanation for the apparently reckless expenditure on your offices.

If this date or time is inconvenient please let me know. Otherwise we will motor through and be on your mat a week on Friday. I take it you will be able to give us a cup of tea?

God Bless and God Forgive You
Mrs Roberta Caldwell-Smyth

4 Newyearfield Farm
Hawk Brae
Ladywell West
Livingston EH54 6TW

8th November 2002

Ms Roberta Caldwell-Smyth
Editor – Church Newsletter
101 Boghall St
Glasgow G69 1DS

Dear Ms Caldwell-Smyth

Thank you for your letter regarding my office allowances. As you
are not a constituent I would not normally respond on such
matters. However, given your gross misunderstanding of the
situation I feel I have to set matters straight.

The sum of £18,000 to which you refer is the cost related to the
running of my constituency office in Livingston. It covers such
items as rent, rates, telephone bills, heating, lighting and burglar
alarm.

My office is situated in central Livingston and is close to many bus
routes, making it easily accessible to my constituents. Crucially, it
is on the ground floor, has full disabled access with disabled toilets,
wide doors to accommodate wheelchairs, no kerbs or steps and
ramps leading up to the office. I took the decision that my office
should be as accessible as possible. I trust you will agree.

It is the case that you cannot provide such an office on the cheap.
If you want to be accessible to constituents then you have to
provide an office. I presume you are not arguing that to save
money I should locate in a back street, upstairs with no toilets and
no disabled access. This would disenfranchise many of my
constituents and I would regard this as totally unacceptable.

It is also the case that last year I installed a heating system as the
office previously had none and I also installed a burglar alarm.
There are many sensitive documents in the office relating to
personal constituent enquiries as well as valuable equipment. It is

only right and proper that I took steps to protect the premises.

In addition, I moved to my current office in the course of the year and as a consequence incurred extra costs over a short period and double rent costs also for a short period. It is also the case that rental levels for premises in Livingston are often significantly higher than in many other parts of Scotland.

In spite of all the above I still remained within my budget. I also must say that, despite my best efforts, I do not recognise my office from your description of sumptuous and palatial.

Given the above I do not see any point in having a meeting but I look forward to receiving an apology.

Yours Sincerely
Bristow Muldoon
MSP for Livingston

101 Boghall St.
Moodiesburn
Glasgow G69 1DS

10th Nov 02

Bristow Muldoon MSP
4 Newyearfield Farm
Hawk Brae
Ladywell West
Livingston EH54 6TW

Dear Mr Muldoon,

You, Sir, are an impudent hound. How dare you demand an apology from members of the public for exercising their citizen's duty to monitor the reprehensible conduct of their elected servants.

The letter you sent to us is risible. Do you seriously expect us to believe that you spend £9,000 more than the average on your 'rented' office because you paid for a 'burglar alarm'!!

You and your party have drowned this country in political sleaze from the 1st of May 1999. First 'Lobbygate' which proved Mr. McConnell is a typical dodgy politician. Then 'Officegate' which proved Mr McLeish was up to his armpits in fiddling his expenses. The parliament building, first advertised as costing £10 million, now according to the Scotsman is approaching the scandalous price of £400 million pounds.

And what of you personally Mr Muldoon? What have you contributed to this first Scottish parliament in 300 years? A deplorable episode of projectile vomiting at a Xmas party for MSPs is your only activity of note for your £50,000 wages. For shame Mr Muldoon.

We enclose five pounds in lieu of the thirty pieces of silver you are due from the Scottish electorate.

God Forgive you
Mrs Roberta Caldwell-Smyth

Bristow Muldoon MSP
Livingston Constituency

12 November 2002

Ms Roberta Caldwell-Smyth
Editor – Church Newsletter
101 Boghall St
Moodiesburn
Glasgow G69 1DS

cc   Mr Eric Bryson
      Rev. Andrew-Derek Roger

Dear Ms Caldwell-Smyth

Having received your letter of the 10th November I have to advise you that it is the nastiest piece of correspondence I have ever received.

That it comes from someone who advises me that she is the Editor of a church Newsletter amazes me.

I see no point in continuing any further correspondence, however I return your £5 which you enclosed with the letter.

Yours sincerely

Bristow Muldoon
MSP for Livingston

From: Hannay Rosemary
To: Elaine.Murray.msp@scottish.parliament.uk
Subject: Holyrood Programme
Sent: Thurs, 6 Sep 2001

Hi Elaine,

I watched you on TV yesterday. I was proud to have you as my MSP. Unfortunately, that glaikit article, John McAllion sitting behind you, pulled a series of grotesque expressions. It is difficult to know if he was doing it on purpose or if he is just an awful eejit.

Elaine, don't sit in front of dopey colleagues if you intend to speak!

The other delicate issue I want to raise with you is a little ticklish. I am nearly 80 years of age and have been in the Labour Party for over forty years. I am a feminist and I hope you will take the advice of an old comrade in the spirit in which it is given. It's your present coiffure. It makes you look like you're wearing Wurzel Gummige's spare heid. My husband said, 'If that's the state her hair is in, I'd hate to see the condition of her hedge!'

Take a leaf out of Wendy's book. She, like you can come across as a little excitable, strident even, but her tidy wee bob can often trick the public into thinking she has command of her brief. Even when she is chattering away incomprehensibly like a gibbon on acid she still exudes gravitas.

Please let me know that you haven't taken offence at the well-meant comments of a silver surfer?

Dr. Rosemary Hannay

From: Elaine.Murray.msp@scottish.parliament.uk
To: Rosemary Hannay
Subject: RE: Holyrood Programme
Sent: 9 Sep 2001

Dear Comrade,

Thank you for your letter – I haven't taken offence! Unfortunately I have been cursed with extremely curly hair which I have great difficulty in straightening despite my most valiant efforts. And I don't have time to sit in a hairdresser's on a regular basis! My hope is to grow it long enough to tie back.

As for McAllion, I fortunately was unable to see what he was up to (there are times it is better not to have eyes in the back of one's head and this may be one).

I am glad you told me – I shall make sure I'm not sitting in front of him next time. McAllion generally uses his contributions to give succour to the SNP and then wonders why he is not asked to speak on behalf of the Executive.

Hope you continue to enjoy Holyrood

Elaine

101 Boghall St.
Moodiesburn
Glasgow
G69 1DS

24 Nov 02

Cathy Peattie MSP
Suite 9 5 Kerse Rd.
Grangemouth FK3 8HQ

Dear Cathy,

Bravo!! I have just watched your diminutive but heroic figure
shuffling out of your local fire station shoulder to shoulder
with the striking pickets. Well done.

Unsurprisingly, as a New Labour MSP on a picket line, you
looked a little awkward and inexperienced. But to quote Dr.
Johnston (who was referring to a dancing dog), 'it is not done
well but one is surprised to see it done at all'.

Of course, sadly, that's your career in politics finished. I think
you will agree that Dr. Simpson's characterisation of the fire-
fighters as 'fascist bastards' is nearer to the prevailing view in
the party than your own principled position.

Your deselection and dumping is only a matter of time. The loss
of your £50,000 salary will come as something of a shock I
imagine. So here's a fiver. Not much I know. But if everyone
sent a fiver who was inspired by your searingly honest
declaration, 'I am ashamed of John Prescott', you could
continue to live in the sybaritic parliamentary style.

The fiver is for you, mind. I don't want it disappearing into one
of Jack's dodgy 'Red Rose Dinner' type accounts and being used
by local drug dealers for their nefarious activities.

All the best to you Cathy and I hope you quickly find alternative
employment.

Yours sincerely
Roberta Caldwell-Smyth

Don't Vote for an Idiot, Vote for a Clown

Roberta Caldwell-Smyth
101 Boghall St.
Moodiesburn
Glasgow G69 1DS

6 December 2002

Dear Roberta,

Thank you for letter of 24th November. I may be diminutive at 5ft 2ins but I was proud to walk (not shuffle) out of Falkirk Fire Station with the striking fire-fighters. Since then I have also been on the picket line at the other fire station within my constituency, at Bo'ness.

I am not sure that I can agree about your quotation from Dr. Johnson and sincerely hope that you are not comparing me to a dancing dog or a Pavlovian one for that matter. I am more of a cat lover. Anyway it was Harold Wilson who said that every dog is allowed one bite.

I would dispute that I looked a little awkward or inexperienced. I have been involved, all my working life, in the trade union movement having been a shop steward. At present I am the convener of the Trades Union Group of MSPs.

I have to tell you that my position is shared by the majority of Labour MSPs and, is more in keeping with the views of ordinary Party members than those expressed by Richard Simpson.

I really appreciate your concern for me, but I can re-assure you that I am not about to be de-selected. I will be the Scottish Labour Party Candidate for Falkirk East at the elections in 2003. I hope that the electorate will have as much faith in me as you seem to have. Perhaps I could persuade you to support my election campaign.

Your donation of a fiver presents something of a dilemma. Should I return it? Should I indulge myself with some delicious chocolate or maybe place a bet on 'Jack The Lad'? Perhaps I should declare it to the parliamentary authorities; after all you might be an undercover reporter for the Daily Mail or the Sun.

Heaven forbid! Anyway this is the season of goodwill, so I will thank you for your best wishes and hope that you have a peaceful Christmas and a Guid New Year.

Yours sincerely
Cathy Peattie MSP

PS. Please find enclosed one fiver returned.

Roberta Caldwell-Smyth
101 Boghall St.
Moodiesburn
Glasgow G69 1DS

11th Dec. 2002

Cathy Peattie MSP
5 Kerse Road
Grangemouth FK3 8HQ

Dear Cathy,

I would indeed be delighted to help in your election campaign. I can't wait to get on the knocker and tell the punters, 'The First Minister says the fire-fighters strike is 'unacceptable' but Cathy Peattie MSP says Jack (Lobbygate/Red Rose Dinner Account) McConnell is a dodgy, right wing, bampot who is a disgrace to the Labour Movement.' The truth always goes down well on the doorstep!

I presume it will be OK to inform the public that the New Parliament building which was originally estimated at 10 million quid, by the Scottish Office under that scoundrel Dewar, is now out of control and to cost them the stupendous figure of, wait for it, . . . at least 400,000,000 quid? That McConnell was caught during the Lobbygate scandal allowing Yankee carpetbaggers, who wanted to invest in lucrative PFI projects, to put appointments directly into his constituency diary and then burnt the diary when the parliament's Standards Ctte.

asked to see it. That Henry McLeish was caught fiddling his office expenses and had to resign in disgrace even though the morons in the Lib/Lab coalition were quite willing to continue supporting the poltroon as First Minister.

Cathy, I have just interrupted this letter to call the Fire Brigades Union and spoke to a Mr Robertson and he informs me that only yourself and Elaine Smith MSP went anywhere near the picket lines in Scotland. So my assertion that most Labour MSPs concur with Richard Simpson MSP that the fire-fighters are 'Fascist Bastards' is conclusively proved.

Why is it that you and Elaine have never been offered any promoted post in the executive? Either, you are a couple of witless, inarticulate simpletons only there to make up the numbers, sookin' sweeties on the back benches, or your principled politics is held against you. The answer, I suggest, is obvious!

I was a little discombobulated to discover you are a cat lover. Every cat lover I ever knew was an imbecilic, psychopathic narcissist, i.e. a Tory. Perhaps this is why you are able to stomach being in the same party with the odious, bewhiskered Richard Simpson MSP!

OK, where do you want me for the campaign, Cathy? Say the word and I will be there!! Let's Go!!!

Roberta Caldwell-Smyth

101 Boghall St
Moodiesburn
Glasgow G69 1DS

24/05/02

RT HON DR JOHN REID MP
Hamilton North and Bellshill Constituency
154 Montrose Cres.
Hamilton ML3 6LL

Dear John,

Did you see last night's 'Question Time' with that dreadful, naive woman Clare Short. When asked, by Dimbleby, if she would have accepted the £100,000 from the proprietor of Express newspapers she said, 'No, I hate pornography'. She went on to say that everything in life, including donations to political parties from pornographers, must be judged from a moral point of view.

Since you, as government spokesman, have been saying you would not sit in moral judgement on donations to the Labour Party, this tacit criticism from a cabinet colleague is intolerable. It makes you look like a moral imbecile and sleazebag willing to accept money from Satan himself!

What Ms. Short fails to understand is the realpolitic of modern political funding. She is happy to accept money from arms dealers (the Hindujas), tobacco interests (indirectly the Ecclestone Formula 1 affair) and plenty of dodgy businessmen (Powderjet, Mittal, Geoffrey Robinson, i.e. 370,000 for Peter Mandelson, etc.) but baulks at a little soft porn. A harmless, and as you have pointed out, entirely legal activity.

John, can nothing be done about this loose cannon's attempts to tarnish the reputation of the Party? Can you assure me that you will continue do everything to raise finance for the Labour Party in spite of Clare Short's mediaeval Presbyterian beliefs?

Yours Sincerely
Asinder Khan

RT HON DR JOHN REID MP
Hamilton North and Bellshill Constituency
154 Montrose Cres.
Hamilton ML3 6LL

12 June 2002

Mr Asinder Khan
101 Boghall St
Moodiesburn
Glasgow G69 1DS

Dear Mr Khan

I write to acknowledge receipt of your recent correspondence to
The Rt Hon Dr John Reid MP.

Dr Reid is out of the office on Ministerial business at the
present time, but I will pass your correspondence to him on his
return.

In the meantime, thank you for taking the time to write.

Best wishes.
Yours sincerely
Connie Mezynski
Secretary

101 Boghall St
Moodiesburn
Glasgow G69 1DS

25 Oct 02

Rt. Hon Dr. John Reid MP
154 Montrose Cres.
Hamilton ML3 6LL

Dear Dr. Reid,

Has your attention been drawn to the unspeakable attack on your probity which appeared in this morning's Scottish Daily Mail? That grotesque reptile, Tim Luckhurst, has written a monstrous piece, on your elevation to Chairman of the Labour Party, which is clearly actionable.

He calls you, 'cunning. . . ruthless. . . New Labour's philosopher thug. . . a hardman Svengali'. He points out that you joined the Communist party in 1973. The blatant sub-text, which no one will miss, is that you joined after the murderous suppression of the Hungarian uprising in 1956 and after the Soviet invasion of Czechoslovakia in 1968 to crush the Prague Spring. The transparent implication being that you are some unreconstructed old 'Stalinist Tankie'.

If there was any doubt he then continues, 'But Reid's critics fear him enough to remain anonymous. Their central accusation is that he is an amoral opportunist and bully, a man who would have been happy to run the KGB if he had been appointed to a Politburo instead of a Cabinet.'

Luckhurst continues, 'He was heavily criticised by the Commissioner for Parliamentary Standards, Elizabeth Filkin, for using his Parliamentary allowance to subsidise political activity.

'And there is evidence that he used tactics of blunt intimidation, sending emissaries with threats to ensure that witnesses to his wrongdoing did not testify to the Parliamentary Committee which let him off the hook.'

This is infamous stuff. I'm surprised he didn't air the old chestnut that you threatened to stiffen Donald Dewar at the Brighton Conference.

Dr. Reid, do you intend to pursue litigation against the Mail? If not, it is my intention to mount a one-man picket outside their Glasgow offices, with a banner proclaiming, RT HON DR JOHN REID MP IS NO THUG, until a retraction is issued. I would be grateful if you could let me know your intentions on this matter.

Yours Sincerely
Asinder Khan

101 Boghall St.
Moodiesburn
Glasgow G69 1DS

13 Aug 2002

Euan Robson MSP
Deputy Minister for Parliamentary Business

Dear Euan,

As a relatively new party member I am usually happy to peruse reports of the activities of our MSPs.

Imagine my consternation on finding, in last week's 'Sunday Times', a damning report on you which claimed: 'There is a version of e-mail that allows the sender to see when the message has been opened or deleted by the recipient. Just such an acknowledgement was received by an SNP researcher last Friday. . . the original e-mail to Robson (was) sent in May 2000, a full 27 months ago.'

For 27 months you had a communication and you did nothing about it!?! How do you think this makes the party look to the public? I'll tell you. It makes us look like a bunch of indolent, incompetent shysters!!

'On Friday (the e-mail) was 'deleted without being read' by someone in Robson's office.' The question immediately suggests itself, 'How many other letters has this poltroon simply dumped?' I consoled myself that few would read this shameful report and others soon forget it. I was confounded to find on opening this week's edition that you have foolishly chosen to continue this disreputable farce.

Euan, if you think claiming that you have been having a little trouble with your IT can excuse 27 months of sloth you must have come up the Clyde in a banana boat. Get the finger out man! You're a Lib Dem for crying out loud, try and act like one! Can you assure me that no other correspondence has been summarily ditched?
Yours Sincerely Rupert Clubbs

NO REPLY

165

From: Archie Beatty
To: mike.rumbles.msp@scottish.parliament.uk
Subject: tuition fees on the doorstep
Sent: 10 May 2001

Hi Mike,

I am a Lib Dem supporter in Aberdeen. I have just been canvassed by a New Labour acolyte and am writing to tell you about the dirty tricks they are getting up to.

The conversation at my front door started in a civilised manner when he asked me to give one example of the Liberals doing anything useful. I said the abolition of tuition fees.

He said 'What would you do if you got on a bus and proffered your fare only to be told that fares had been abolished. You go up stairs, smoke a cigarette and at your destination you prepare to alight only to be asked for your fare?

He said, 'You would call the driver a Lying Lib Dem B_____d'.

I was very upset (I'm 75) by the bad language especially as I couldn't think of anything to counter his filthy lie.

Could you drop me a wee line saying what you would have done in my position?

Yours Etc.
Archie Beatty

PS. My Granddaughter Amelia showed me how to send this e-mail it's my first time!

From: mike.rumbles.msp@scottish.parliament.uk
To: Archie Beatty
Subject: RE: tuition fees on the doorstep
Sent: Thurs, 10 May 2001

Dear Archie,

Thanks for your e-mail. It is useful to know what our opponents are doing and I, like you, deplore the way in which this canvasser spoke to you. Without doubt the Lib Dems have forced Labour into doing things it didn't want to do, we have abolished tuition fees – I would have asked him whether he knew of any Scottish students who had to pay £1,075 this year to access their course. (Answer – none of course!)

Other things we have achieved (To name just a few) the re-introduction of student grants for the poorest students, the commitment to give free personal care for the elderly (against Labour wishes), and an enhanced package for our teachers – the envy of that available south of the border.

There is no doubt in my mind that we have been a civilising influence on the Labour Party in the Scottish Parliament and they don't like it! I'm confident that the voters will recognise this in the election.

Hope this e-mail has been helpful,
With Best Wishes
Mike Rumbles

From: Archie Beatty
Sent: Thurs, 10/05/01 14:32
To: Mike.rumbles.msp@scottish.parliament.uk
Subject: RE: tuition fees on the doorstep

Hi Mike,
Thanks for a very swift reply. I have found out that the big lad who was so rude lives round the corner. I would like to engage him again on tuition fees. Your answer was helpful but could you say something specifically about the analogy he makes about being asked for your fare as you get off the bus. That's the bit that really stumped me. Once I have your reply I intend to go round to his door and whisker him one on the snout with my aluminium walking stick.

Yours Etc.
Archie Beatty

Don't Vote for an Idiot, Vote for a Clown

From: mike.rumbles.msp@scottish.parliament.uk
To: Archie Beatty
Subject: RE: tuition fees on the doorstep
Sent: Thurs, 10 May 2001

Dear Archie,

I'd be equally blunt with him, I'd say unfortunately bus fares haven't been abolished for everyone, only those who live north of the border! I've been given a free bus pass by the Scottish Executive (at the insistence of the Lib Dems) and isn't it about time the Labour Party provided such a free pass for everyone throughout the UK.

On the serious issue of the student endowment I wouldn't confuse this with the abolition of the £3,075 of tuition fees, the Scottish Executive has agreed to pay into an endowment fund to help our poorest students with grants and this will be ring-fenced money. 50% of graduates who have completed their courses (and who, remember, have benefitted by having their tuition fees paid in full by the Scottish Executive) will be exempt from contributing £2,000 into this fund – which will start to be repaid when they are earning. Thus, at a stroke the barrier to accessing higher education has been fully removed and grants restored for our poorest students. This is a major achievement gained in the teeth of Labour opposition.

Of the many other achievements you could list, the committment to free personal care for the elderly, the better deal for our teachers and the proposals for a much more robust freedom of information Bill.

Regards,
Mike

From: Archie Beatty
Sent: 10 May 2001 23:13
To: Mike.Rumbles.msp@scottish.parliament.uk
Subject: Bus Fares and tuition fees

Hello again Mike,

I took your advice and went round to his house and was extremely blunt. So much so that he tried to push me off his doorstep. One thing led to another and to cut a long story short I gave him a couple of dull ones with my stick. We think he has concussion.

His mother called the police and I have been charged with breach of the peace and assault. I explained to the policewoman that you had recommended that I be blunt. She had never heard of you, and at first thought I was making up your name, but said you must be some kind of bampot and you were a disgrace to the parliament.

I am sorry I gave your name and I hope you won't get into trouble with the papers over this. The station sergeant says I'll probably get community service because of my age but he thinks that by rights it should be the MSP who provoked the assault who should really serve the sentence.

The sad thing is that in my heart I think the big lad from the Labour party is probably right and that students are being asked for their fare as they leave the bus.

Yours Etc.
Archie

From: mike.rumbles.msp@scottish.parliament.uk
Sent: Wed. 16/05/01 13:16
To: 'Archie Beatty'
Subject: RE: Busfares and tuition fees

Dear Archie,

It's been fun corresponding with you, hope you had similar enjoyment.

Regards,
Mike

From: Rosemary Hannay [mailto:hannayrosemary@hotmail.com]
Sent: 08 August 2001 14:27
To: michael.russell.msp@scottish.parliament.uk
Subject: Tory MSPs

Dear Mike Russell,

In the early 70s I was, to my eternal shame, a member of the Young Conservatives in Girvan. A prominent contemporary was one Philip Gallie. We were never close associates but we did move in the same cultural milieu.

To cut a long story short, I recently had my old Beta Max cassettes upgraded to VHS and during the process came across some old footage of fund raising events organised by the Federation of Conservative Students (FCS). Not to put too fine a point on it they contain some fairly rude scenes featuring two now prominent male Tory MSPs in their cups. (Not a pretty sight even then!)

Since friend Gallie is the official spokesperson on group sex I think you (and perhaps John Swinney) should have a look at this. As it happens I will be in Edinburgh next Monday and will drop a copy into your office at the Parliament.

Dr. Rosemary Hannay

PS. If you are not there can your staff be trusted not to broadcast this stuff all over Holyrood?

From: Michael.Russell.msp@scottish.parliament.uk
To: 'Rosemary Hannay' hannayrosemary@hotmail.com
Subject: RE: Tory MSPs
Date: Sun, 12 Aug 2001 09:37:11 +0100

Thanks for this.

I have been away on holiday and am only just making my way through my in box. I am unfortunately not in the office on Monday but my Parliamentary Assistant Dr Alasdair Allan will be here and his discretion is absolute.

I look forward (perhaps not quite the right term) to seeing the tape.

Michael

From: Roberta Caldwell-Smyth
Sent: 03 October 2002 09:25
To: mary.scanlon.msp@scottish.parliament.uk
Subject: mock school election

Hi Mary,
My thirteen year old son, Raymond, has been selected to represent the Tory party in a mock election at his school in Inverness. His father and I were quietly pleased and not a little proud as we are staunch supporters of the party.

However, we were astounded when we discovered what his modern studies teacher told him about his candidature. She said, 'As a Tory you should promote family values and public probity while being like all the rest of them, corrupt, mendacious and hypocritical.'

We had arranged an interview to complain to the headmistress before this 'stushie' about Mr Major and Mrs Currie hit the ventilation system. We feel any complaint must now be risible.

I really don't know what to do for the best. We feel that the only solution is for Raymond to withdraw his candidature but this will leave no Conservative presence. Mary, can you suggest anything in the circumstances?
Regards
Roberta Caldwell-Smyth

From: Mary.Scanlon.msp@scottish.parliament.uk
To: Roberta Caldwell-Smyth
Subject: RE: mock school election
Sent: Thurs, 3 Oct 2002

Can I ask what school your son attends? I do not think that it is acceptable for a teacher to take this line. I appreciate that the teacher's remark has made it very difficult for Raymond but I do hope that he will endure.

I would be pleased to take this matter up with the Headmaster and the Director of Education. If nothing is said then the same teacher will continue this approach for years to come. I would be happy to take the matter forward – but not to mention that you raised it with me. Please let me know what I can do to help. Thank you for letting me know about this.
MARY

Don't Vote for an Idiot, Vote for a Clown

From: Roberta Caldwell-Smyth
To: Mary Scanlon
Subject: RE: mock school election
Sent: Thurs, 03 Oct 2002

Hi Mary,

Thanks for your prompt response. As you will appreciate I am extremely reluctant to allow my son's name or his school to be dragged through the mire on this.

You very kindly said you would be willing to take this up with the Director of Education but we are unclear as to how you could reasonably tackle this after the unsavoury and salacious revelations of Edwina Currie. It is further complicated by the unheard of deceitfulness and cant of John Major.

If you combine this with the tawdry activities of Jonathan Aitken MP (18 months), Chief Secretary to the Treasury, Lord Jeffrey Archer (2 years) Deputy Chairman of the Conservative party and Neil Hamilton MP (hanging would be too good for him), a challenge to the outburst of my son's teacher would seem problematic.

The insalubrious adventures of David Mellor MP, Tim Yeo MP, Piers Merchant MP, Stephen Milligan MP (he of the suspenders and soft fruit), Michael Brown MP (took an under age young man on holiday with him), David Ashby MP (putatively shared a bed with another man in a hotel 'to save money'), Steven Norris MP (reputed to have at least 5 mistresses), Nicholas Fairbairn MP, Alan Clark MP, etc., etc. ad nauseam, makes it difficult to see how you could take up this case with the Director of Education without appearing disingenuous.

If you could convince me that any defence is feasible I would be willing to proceed but not if we are all just to become a laughing stock.

Regards
Roberta Caldwell-Smyth

From: Mary.Scanlon.msp@scottish.parliament.uk
To: Roberta Caldwell-Smyth
Subject: RE: mock school elections
Sent: Mon, 07 Oct 2002

Dear Roberta

What can I say? The list goes on. I cannot even start to defend the shameful behaviour of the individuals you listed. I will not list the offenders in the other main party as it does not add anything to the debate.

I do fully understand that you would not wish your name associated with the problem. I have not asked you which school your son attended or indeed your home address in order to ensure confidentiality.

I will however drop a line to Bruce Robertson as I believe that he will be concerned at the 'intimidating' effect of teachers on young people's politics.

Personally, I do my best to work hard in the Highlands and in Edinburgh to win back trust and confidence in my Party – it is not helped when revelations about Edwina Currie and John Major come to light, particularly when I have been made to feel 'inferior' in the past because my marriage failed and of course was classed as a single parent.

I am very grateful to you for bringing this issue to my attention.
My best wishes,
Mary Scanlon

Don't Vote for an Idiot, Vote for a Clown

From: Mary.Scanlon.msp@scottish.parliament.uk
To: Roberta Caldwell-Smyth
Subject: RE: mock school elections
Sent: Tues, 15 Oct 2002

Dear Mrs Caldwell-Smyth

Please find attached a copy of the letter that Mary Scanlon has sent to Arthur McCourt. The emails that were sent had any reference to the school or your son blanked out.

Please do not hesitate to contact Mary Scanlon if you have any further queries.

Kind Regards,
Lucy Harington, Assistant to Mary Scanlon MSP

Arthur McCourt
Chief Executive
Highland Council
Glenurquhart Road
Inverness IV3 5NX

14 October 2002

I enclose copies of emails which are self-explanatory.
I am very supportive of youth voice and encouraging pupils to enter into the political sphere. Indeed, I recently visited Millburn Academy with Rhoda Grant MSP and Fergus Ewing MSP. We had an excellent 'hustings' with pupils and a further meeting for questions from pupils. The whole exercise was very enjoyable and all MSPs were warmly welcomed by staff and pupils, including the Headmaster, Graeme Spence.
I am very alarmed at the intimidating approach taken by the teacher and headmistress involved in the case enclosed. The family do not wish their son, his teacher, or the school to be mentioned and I have taken measures to ensure confidentiality.
I would like to ask the Highland Council to ensure that pupils who wish to represent every party are given the opportunity to do so without fear of bullying and intimidation by teachers or fear of pupils being 'pilloried or ridiculed by contemporaries' believing that this behaviour would be in line with the teacher's views.
I further ask that the democratic right of free speech be encouraged throughout Highland Schools.

Arthur McCourt
Chief Executive
Highland Council
Glenurquhart Road
Inverness IV3 5NX

15 November 2002

Mrs Mary Scanlon MSP
Constituency Office-
37 Ardconnel Terrace
Inverness IV23AE

Dear Mary

Mock Political School Elections

I refer to your letter dated 14 October 2002 in connection with concems that you raised regarding a recent mock political school election in which your constituent alleged that their child was intimidated by a modern studies teacher and headteacher to withdraw as a Conservative candidate.

As you will appreciate it is difficult to undertake an investigation into an allegation of this nature without having more information. Nevertheless I would be particularly disappointed if it was found to be accurate, especially as the Highland Council, in partnership with the Highland Wellbeing Alliance is committed to creating increased opportunities for young people to become involved in their communities, in service development and in the decision making processes.

Indeed as you are aware, a major initiative that the Council has been closely involved with has been the establishment of the Highland Youth Voice. This elected body of young people is drawn from every area of Highland and enables them to have a wide range of opportunities to 'have their say' and are also involved in taking forward their own agenda and tackling issues that are important to them.

I would like to assure you that The Highland Council firmly believes in the democratic right of each individual to freely express their views and to represent whatever political party they wish.

I have discussed this matter with the Director of Education Culture and Sport and asked him to remind staff of the importance of treating all views in an impartial and fair manner when undertaking mock political school elections.

I would like to take this opportunity to thank you for the time that you and other politicians have given to attend school meetings to both support mock political school elections and encourage young people's awareness of the democratic process.

Yours Sincerely

Arthur D McCourt
Chief Executive

101 Boghall St
Moodiesburn
Glasgow G69 1DS

21 November 2002

Mary Scanlon MSP
37 Arconnel Terrace
Inverness IV2 3AE

Dear Mrs Scanlon,

On behalf of my parents and myself I would like to thank you for your efforts on my behalf. However, after much research and no little soul searching I have decided not to represent the Conservatives in the mock elections in my school.

I do not feel I could support a party which still reveres Margaret Thatcher, a crazed war criminal responsible for the deaths of 368 men and boys in the Belgrano. I refuse to represent a party which callously destroyed the coal industry in this country and left the NHS to flounder for 18 long years. I would be sickened to my stomach to be involved with a party which espouses 'family values' but which is a sewer of sleaze both sexual and financial. (Only this week we find that Mr Sebastion Coe MP has left his wife and 4 young children for a 'floosy'.)

I have just read Edwina Currie's frank and revealing diaries. Her revelations about her affair with Mr Major and his 'large blue underpants' are utterly nauseating. The picture she paints of a party of halfwits, incompetents and sybarites is truly loathsome.

How you, Mrs Scanlon, obviously a lady of some sensitivity, can bear to belong to this noisome amalgam of rapacious liars and reckless hedonists beggars belief. Your party is financed and sustained by plutocrats, a mediaeval aristocracy and hordes of snobs and toadies.

Mrs Scanlon, ask yourself how people like Jeffrey Archer, Jonathan Aitken and John Major can get to the top of your party and remain there for decades? I hope you will emulate the actions of Winston Churchill and cross the floor to the Lib Dems. (They are after all just Tories without the low cunning.)

Forward to the Socialist Republic!
Raymond Caldwell-Smyth (9)

Don't Vote for an Idiot, Vote for a Clown

From: Rosemary Hannay hannayrosemary@hotmail.com
Sent: 05 September 2001 11:36
To: tavish.scott.msp@scottish.parliament.uk
Subject: PR

Hi Tavish,

I heard you on Radio Scotland this morning. You came over as very accomplished and well informed. Well done. Not like the Tory who sounded like a wishy washy balloon.

Tavish, I have just joined the party and attended my first branch meeting last night. I innocently inquired if we had any plans to capitalise on the imminent introduction of PR in Local Government. I was met by a vulgar wave of snorts and guffaws (that is if five people in a room can generate a wave).

It turns out that none of our branch expects the executive to deliver PR inspite of the commitment in the 'Programme for Government' document. When I averred that we could depend on Jim Wallace and Ross to push it through the chairperson said 'get real, Rosemary'. I am shocked at this debilitating cynicism. Please tell me it's not true! We can depend on getting PR before the next election can't we?

Dr. Rosemary Hannay

PS. If only you hadn't made such a haddie of the fishing issue I'm sure you would be our next leader in Scotland! Still a week's a long time in politics.

From: tavish.scott.msp@scottish.parliament.uk
To: Rosemary Hannay
Subject: PR
Sent: Thurs, 6 Sep 2001

Dear Dr Hannay
Thank you for your message. The Parliamentary Party are committed to voting reform for local government. Indeed the First Minister said yesterday in response to Iain Smith that the Executive were committed to delivering the principles of the Kerley Committee, which of course advocated a PR system of STV. That is what we are working hard to achieve.

Regards, Tavish Scott

From: hannayrosemary@hotmail.com
Sent: 06 September 2001 22:07
To: tavish.scott.msp@Scottish.parliament.uk

Subject: PR in Local Government

Hi Tavish,

Many thanks for your swift reply to my e-mail. I showed your message to some members of our branch tonight (we were having a social to raise party funds).

I am sorry to inform you that your explanation was greeted with the same misanthropic glee. 'Tavish is talkin' tosh,' said Mike our Chairperson. Susan, our treasurer, claimed, 'If you believe that guff from Tavish you'll believe anything, Rosemary'. 'Not a snowball's,' said Arthur Beatty an elderly gentleman.

Look Tavish, if I've got to defend the party in public I need to have a realistic assessment of the situation. My daughter is at Strathclyde Uni. and already denounces me for joining 'a bunch of wishy washy, middle class, w_____s'!! What are the real chances of us forcing the Labour party to grant PR in local government? Fifty/ Fifty? Sixty/ Forty? One in a hundred?

At the social they were saying we had as much chance of getting PR as Craig Brown leading Scotland into the 2006 World Cup i.e. none. Given the debatable veracity of our claim to have abolished tuition fees, if we don't get PR it will look suspiciously like we really are a load of useless shysters.

(Tonight they were joking – Question: What do you call a bus driver who, when you get on the bus tells you that fares have been abolished, but when you try to get off demands the fare? Answer: A lying Lib Dem B_____d!)

Ok, we can't tell the public but I really feel you must be brutally candid with party members. Tavish, are we going to get it or not? Simple question! Will you give me a simple answer?

Rosemary Hannay

From: tavish.scott.msp@scottish.parliament.uk
To: Rosemary Hannay
Subject: RE:PR in Local Government
Sent: Sat, 8 Sep 2001

Rosemary

Could you send in the name of your local branch, and we can see from within the Parliamentary Party who could attend a meeting to discuss this matter.

I am not clear as to which constituency you are writing from.

Regards
Tavish Scott

101 Boghall St.
Moodiesburn
Glasgow G69 1DS

13/05/02

Dear Elaine Smith MSP,

I was astounded to see in my 'Herald' today that you are one of only 8 Labour MSPs (out of 54) yet to be offered a promotion or job in the parliament. They quoted David McLetchie the Tory leader as suggesting the remaining eight were so incompetent, so useless that even their own party feared to entrust them with any responsibility.

I have discussed this slight on our area with many of my customers in the post office and the consensus is that their local MSP must indeed be a nincompoop!

I bridle at this insult to the people of this locality and to you personally. I've argued that you must be very young or inexperienced and that we can expect that your career will soar when you are given half a chance. Unfortunately, I haven't really convinced myself.

Could you drop me a line suggesting why you have been overlooked by your colleagues so that I may defend our local MSP against the apathetic cynics who use my shop.

Yours Sincerely
Asinder Khan

Mr Khan
101 Boghall St.
Moodiesburn G69 1DS

20th May 2002

Dear Mr Khan

Letter Dated 13th May 2002

Thank you for your letter of 13th May 2002. I'm always happy to hear from my constituents and respond to them.

As you might be aware the Scottish Parliament is a much smaller institution than Westminster, with only 129 MSPs of various political parties and two independents.

The Labour Party, the main party of the coalition government, has 55 MSPs. The Executive at present is made up of 10 ministers and 10 deputy ministers, 16 labour and 4 liberal democrats. These are 'paid' positions, i.e. they receive a larger salary than a backbench member.

Certain unfortunate circumstances have meant Executive re-shuffles. Firstly, the unexpected sudden, sad death of Donald Dewar. His successor, Henry McLeish re-shuffled the cabinet to bring in a few new faces. Unfortunately, Henry McLeish felt obliged to resign from his position last November and the new First Minister, Jack McConnell, re-shuffled the Cabinet quite substantially. Had Donald Dewar still been First Minister, then there would likely have been minimal change.

The other positions that this article refers to are the unpaid posts of Committee Conveners or vice-conveners and the new positions, also unpaid, of Ministerial Parliamentary Aids.

At present, I have no ambition to hold a cabinet position or any unpaid post. I am a member of a number of cross-party groups and serve on two committees and I am the Equal Opportunities Committee Gender Reporter. I have accepted an invitation to join the board of the South Coatbridge Social Inclusion Partnership.

The role of backbench MSPs in the governing parties is important since I believe they have a particular job to do in questioning the Executive and holding them to account. I believe that I can best serve my constituents in this way at the present time.

To specifically answer a point you make, I do not think I am particularly young, but I do live in my constituency, I was born and brought up here, and I am married with a young son. I believe this helps me to understand and empathise with many of the issues affecting my constituents.

In terms of being inexperienced, no MSP had any experience of a Scottish Parliament, or how it would operate, since it was a brand new institution.

To help you reassure your customers that I am working on their behalf, I have enclosed copies of my last two annual reports. I will send you this year's when it is produced. I have also enclosed some surgery leaflets that you might be kind enough to display in your shop. Anyone with internet access can also find information on my website at http://www.elaine.co.uk

I deal with hundreds of constituents and take my responsibilities in representing them very seriously indeed.

If I can be of further assistance, or if you would like me to visit your premises and speak to your customers, please get in touch with my constituency office to arrange a mutually convenient date and time.

Thank you again for your correspondence.

Yours sincerely
Elaine Smith MSP

Don't Vote for an Idiot, Vote for a Clown

From: Archie Beatty [mailto:snash@maxies.fsnet.co.uk]
Sent: 09 May 2001 16:29
To: presiding.officer@scottish.parliament.uk
Subject: Parliament building

Hi Lord Steel,

I am one of your constituents in Tweeddale and a staunch Liberal. Have you seen today's Scotsman? They are seeking to publicly humiliate you over the overspend on the parliament.

I may be able to help. I have been contacted by some 'friends' who wish to remain anonymous. (They are, shall we say, of an extraterrestrial nature but I hope you will keep that under your hat.)

They will be able to help avoid an electoral disaster over this.

I'll be in Edinburgh next Thursday and I'll come up to your office with one of them to discuss things.

Yours Etc.
Archie Beatty

From: David.McLaren@scottish.parliament.uk
Sent: Wed. 09/05/01 18.33
To: snash@maxies.fsnet.co.uk
Subject: RE: Parliament building

Sir David was grateful for your e-mail and has asked me to respond.

Whilst he is grateful for your support on the Holyrood issue, he is I am afraid unfortunately unable to meet with you to discuss this as you suggest in your message.

You might like to know that Sir David is no longer MP for the Tweeddale constituency.

Regards.

David McLaren
Private Secretary

From: Archie Beatty
Sent: 10 May 2001 09:53
To: David.McLaren@scottish.parliament.uk
Subject: RE: Parliament building

Hi David Mclaren,

David, I wasn't entirely candid with you in my last e-mail. I said I was in touch with extraterrestrials because I thought you might not believe me. In fact I have been contacted by Enric Miralles and he has information to counter the David Black book and clear Lord Steel.

(He also says he is going to do for Margo MacDonald and old Gorrie who he blames for the whole fiasco.) I am sure you will appreciate that this changes everything.

So unless I hear from you I'll come into your office next Thursday morning as agreed.

Archie Beatty

From: David.McLaren@scottish.parliament.uk
Sent: Thurs, 10/05/01 11.12
To: snash@maxies.fsnet.co.uk
Subject: RE: Parliament building

Mr Beatty

Thank you for your e-mail. I am sorry but it will not be possible to meet with you on this matter. Sir David is extremely busy, as you might imagine.

If there is any information you wish to impart on this matter please provide it in writing.

David McLaren

From: Archie Beatty [mailto:snash@maxies.fsnet.co.uk]
Sent: 11 May 2001 09:45
To: David. McLaren@scottish. parliament. uk
Subject: 300 million overspend

Mr McLaren,

Well the book was published yesterday and Lord Steel hasn't come out of it smelling of roses. It may still be possible to retrieve something from this whole debacle.

Senor Miralles has told me that it is absolutely vital that we speak to David Steel immediately. We understand that you may be a little sceptical.

So as an indication of our bona fides will you mention to His Lordship a certain incident which only Sir David and Enric could possibly know about, viz. Lord Steel tapped Enric for twenty quid last time he was in Edinburgh and characteristically Mr Steel never repaid it.

See you next Thursday morning as planned, I am looking forward to meeting you.

Yours etc.
Archie Beatty

From: David.McLaren@scottish.parliament.uk
Sent: Fri. 11/05/01
To: snash@maxies.fsnet.co.uk
Subject: RE: 300 million overspend

Mr Beattie

As I have made clear in previous e-mails, it will not be possible to meet with you next Thursday.

David McLaren

To: David.McLaren@scottish.parliament.uk
From: Archie Beatty
Sent: 12/05/01
Subject: Pleasuredome

David McLaren,

To be quite frank I do not like your tone. I wonder if you are even a Lib Dem. You are behaving like a Tory Rottweiller.

You promised me an interview with Lord Steel to try to extricate him from the unholy shambles he has made of the Holyrood project. Now you are trying to wriggle out of your commitment with weasel words unworthy of an amanuensis.

Senor Miralles is not best pleased I can assure you. Will we be welcome in your office next Thursday morning or not?

Archie Beatty

PS. Does Sir David know about this?

From: David.McLaren@scottish.parliament.uk
Sent: Fri. 11/05/01 11:42
To: snash@maxies.fsnet.co.uk
Subject:RE: Senor Miralles Visit

Mr Beattie

In previous e-mails to you I have tried to make it clear that it would not be possible to meet you to discuss this matter. You clearly have evidence to the contrary given your personal criticism of me in your latest e-mail. You might like to let me have a copy of this evidence.

I am sorry that because Sir David is unable to meet you, and my communications to that effect have caused you offence. However, given the tone of your latest e-mail, I do not see any purpose being served in continuing this correspondence.

David McLaren

From: snash@maxies.fsnet.co.uk
Sent: Fri. 11/05/01 12:36
To: David.McLaren@scottish.parliament.uk
Subject: RE: Pleasure Dome

David,

Steady on man. We are both under a lot of pressure. It's no picnic being in contact with the spirit world and I certainly don't envy your position, having to work for the man who has presided over the largest architectural fiasco since Kublai Khan did a stately pleasure dome decree.

Let's say no more about it and I'll pop through your door next Thursday at 10.00pm precisely and Enric will materialise about ten minutes later.

All the best
Archie

From: David.McLaren@scottish.parliament.uk
Sent: Fri. 11/05/01 12:56
To: snash@maxies.fsnet.co.uk
Subject: RE: Pleasure Dome

Your e-mail is acknowledged. As previously indicated there is no possibility of a meeting next Thursday.

David McLaren

101 Boghall St
Moodiesburn
Glasgow G69 1DS

30/06/02

Dear Sir David,

Can I bring to your attention a disgraceful snippet which was published in today's 'Sunday Times'. In the 'Atticus' diary on page 19 it mentions that the Scottish Parliamentary Journalists' Association held its annual dinner last Tuesday and then continued:

'One guest was Lord Steel, the presiding officer, who was spotted leaving the Balmoral Hotel clutching something in his hand. On closer inspection it turned out to be four of the miniatures of whisky left out for diners. So nice of him to tidy up.'

This is a blatant attempt to besmirch your reputation. They are implying that you are a drunk, a thief and, probably more damaging, a cheapskate prepared to creep about tables at a public function harvesting free alcohol.

The probity of an MSP is jealously guarded. This unfounded slander is intended to open you to derision and vilification. It shall not pass uncontested.

It is my intention to picket the News International offices in Glasgow next week protesting about this outrageous political assassination. I have already prepared a banner saying: 'David Steel MSP is no inebriate or thief'. I will remain until an apology is issued. I will, of course, contact the BBC and STV. (My daughter works as a researcher on the Lesley Riddoch show)

Can I tell them that I have your support on this David?

Yours Sincerely
Asinder Khan

The Rt Hon Sir David Steel KBE MSP
The Presiding Officer

3 July 2002

Asinder Khan
101 Boghall St
Moodiesburn
GLASGOW G69 1DS

I am most grateful to you for drawing my attention to the disgraceful piece in the Sunday Times gossip column, which I had not seen. Disgraceful because of the lie that I left the journalists' dinner with four miniatures of whisky. This is totally untrue. It was three. Mine, my wife's and one unwanted by a fellow guest at the table.

I think it is simply called journalistic licence. Good luck with your protest. May you be joined by thousands of outraged readers.

David Steel

101 Boghall St
Moodiesburn
Glasgow G69 1DS

07/07/02

The Scottish Parliament
Adviser to the Standards Committee
Room 5.19 Parliament Headquarters George IV Bridge
Edinburgh EH99 1SP

Dear Mr Rumbles,

I wrote to David Steel on the 30/05/02 concerning a malicious piece in the Sunday Times. It claimed that Sir David had been observed leaving a public function with 4 miniatures of whisky which, they implied, he had stolen.

Imagine my stupefaction on opening my Sunday Times the following week to find sections of my private letter and my name derided in their diary section. Imagine my incredulity in finding them also reproduced and ridiculed in the Sunday Herald diary.

The Sunday Herald's Alan Taylor was happy to tell me that Lord Steel had personally handed him the letter and reply.

Mr. Rumbles, is it acceptable for David Steel, the man who maniacally denounced 'bitch journalism', to leak a private letter from a member of the public to the poisonous reptiles of the Scottish press?

I take it that as the Presiding Officer Mr. Steel is not above the standards of probity that your committee is striving to establish?

Can I take it that you will vigorously investigate this breach of parliamentary etiquette even if it leads to the impeachment of Lord Steel?

Yours Sincerely
Asinder Khan

Don't Vote for an Idiot, Vote for a Clown

The Scottish Parliament
Adviser to the Standards Committee
Room 5.19 Parliament Headquarters
George IV Bridge
Edinburgh EH99 1SP

23 July 2002

Private Confidential

Asinder Khan
101 Boghall St
Moodiesbum
Glasgow G69 1DS

Dear Asinder Khan,

I refer to your letter addressed to Mr Rumbles, and received here on 15 July 2002, which has been passed to me as the Independent Adviser to the Standards Committee of the Scottish Parliament.

My initial responsibility is to determine whether the conduct of MSPs in the course of parliamentary duties amounts to a breach of the Scottish Parliament's Code of Conduct and whether the matter warrants formal investigation. The Code of Conduct can be found at: www. Parliament.uk/msps/coc/coc-c.htrn, but if you do not have access to the internet a paper copy can be provided.

The contents of your letter indicates that your complaint is about the release of a private letter you sent to Sir David Steel, MSP on 30th May 2002. You say that extracts from this letter appeared in the Press and you assert that Sir David Steel had handed the letter and his reply to Alan Taylor of the Sunday Herald. You question whether it is acceptable for David Steel to leak a private letter from a member of the public to the press, and ask whether the matter will be investigated.

It would be helpful if you could confirm that my understanding of your complaint is accurate, and provide any documentation (such as copy letters and the reply received) which you may have relating to the matter.

You refer to 'a breach of parliamentary etiquette' and you should indicate the section of the Code of Conduct you believe to have been breached by the MSP concerned. If I thereafter consider that formal investigation is warranted I will advise you at that stage of the procedures which will follow. On completion of my investigation, I will submit a report to the Standards Committee.

I look forward to your reply,

Yours sincerely,
W.A.Spence
Adviser to the Standards Committee

101 Boghall St
Moodiesburn
Glasgow G69 1DS

25 July 2002

Mr W. A. Spence
Adviser to the Standards Committee
The Scottish Parliament
Edinburgh EH99 1SP

Dear Mr Spence,

I am in receipt of your extraordinary letter of the 23rd. In it you say, 'You refer to a "breach of parliamentary etiquette" and you should indicate the section of the Code of Conduct you believe to have been breached by the MSP concerned.' I should look up the code and tell you where it has been breached?!? What exactly do they pay you for?

I can see what is going on here. Mr Rumbles as a fellow Lib Dem is prevaricating. Lord Steel's behaviour is a clear breach of parliamentary probity which if it reaches the public arena will result in his certain impeachment and public humiliation for their party.

Mr Rumbles hopes to divert me by having you write a complex and confusing missive demanding that I do the spade work. Why doesn't he simply ask David Steel if it is true? Why don't you simply ask Lord Steel if it is true?

As a result of your serpentine ploy to bury this affair I now formally ask you to investigate Mr Rumbles attempts at cover-up and your own less than salubrious part in this sorry affair.

Yours Sincerely
Asinder Khan

The Scottish Parliament
Adviser to the Standards Committee
Room 5.19 Parliament Headquarters George IV Bridge
Edinburgh EH99 1SP

9 August 2002

Mr Andrew S Bain
101 Boghall St
Moodiesburn
Glasgow G69 1DS

Dear Mr Bain,

Complaint by 'Asinder Khan'

I am enclosing some press cuttings which have come to my attention. The cuttings indicate that you may have been using the pseudonym 'Asinder Khan' in recent correspondence with me regarding a complaint against Sir David Steel MSP. A glance at the Electoral Register appears to confirm the press reports.

I am writing to let you know that I do not propose to take any further action in relation to the purported complaint by 'Asinder Khan'. I am copying this letter to the Clerk to the Standards Committee.

Yours sincerely,
W. A. Spence, Adviser to the Standards Com'mittee

From: hannayrosemary@scottish.parliament.uk
To: Jamie.stone.msp@scottish.parliament.uk
Subject: Leadership
Date: Fri, 7 Sep 2001 10:03

Hi Jamie,

I have been asked to write to you by some members in the Cumbernauld branch to see if you would be willing to accept nomination for Party Leader.

We watched Jim Wallace on the Party Political Broadcast yesterday and are convinced that the time has come to challenge his inept leadership. Jim came over as a cross between the Pillsbury doughboy and Goofy. His contention that because we got a few more votes than the Tories at the General Election, we are somehow popular is risible. He is so grey and uninspiring and it is clear he has caved in on PR for Local Government.

You on the other hand, Jamie, would bring a bit of colour to the Party leadership and much needed incisiveness. We know that your exuberant couture has occasionally been characterised as foppish but we prefer to see it as individualistic. We well remember your brave stance on Mike Tyson. Anyone who calls on Glaswegians to throw eggs at Mad Mike, while he is in the same city as you, is either a plain speaking paragon or a reckless lunatic!

The Party needs your plain speaking, your forthrightness and your political sagacity. What do you say? Have we your permission to submit your name as Leader?

Looking forward to hearing from you.

Dr. Rosemary Hannay

From: hughodonnell@cix.co.uk
To: hannayrosemary@hotmail.com
Subject: Leadership
Date: Tues, 18 Sep 2001 17:19

Hello,

I was interested to learn from a mutual acquaintance that some members of the Lib Dems in Cumbernauld had asked you to write to Mr Jamie Stone. I thought I should perhaps contact you in relation to your suggestion that Jamie Stone had been recommended by the Cumbernauld branch of the Lib Dems as prospective leader.

I would be interested in speaking to the Convener of the local party to discuss this issue further and would be obliged if you could tell me the time and location of the next branch meeting. I may even consider joining the Party following such a discussion.

From: hannayrosemary@hotmail.com
To: hughodonnell@cix.co.uk
Subject: Jamie for Leader
Date: Wed, 19 Sep 2001 10:47

Hi Hugh,

I wish you would join the Party! Paying your subscription then sitting on your ample posterior the rest of the year is not what we expect from people who seek to represent the Lib Dems.

I am sorry for the cloak and dagger stuff but candidly you, as a Jim Wallace sycophant, are the last person we would approach. You know perfectly well that I said to Jamie that some of us wanted to sound him out. I did NOT say that he had been nominated by the Cumbernauld branch.

Although it does not surprise us that you attempt to distort and mangle our position to try to sully our names.

Jamie may be outlandish in his attire, (but no more so than Lord

Steel) he may be a fop and unknown outside the party (the same could be said of Tavish Scott) and he may be a little bonkers but when did that ever debar anyone from membership of the Lib Dems? The point is he has charisma. (Something which seems to have been surgically removed from yourself.) He has gravitas. And most importantly in our opinion he has loads of bottom, something sadly lacking in Goofy Wallace's case.

Your sinister e-mail and transparent attempt to unmask us verges on Stalinism. We will not hesitate to go to the press if you try to sabotage our entirely democratic right to seek alternative leadership candidates for the conference!

See You at the next meeting.
Dr. Rosemary Hannay

From: hughodonnell@cix.co.uk
To: hannayrosemary@hotmail.com
Subject: Jamie for Leader
Date: Wed, 19 Sep 2001 13:15

Dear Dr Hannay,

I have been highly entertained by your e mail and would be interested to know the colour of the sky on your planet. Your language and personalised vitriol hardly seem in keeping with either Liberal democracy or someone who claims to be a Dr. I would be quite happy for you to talk to the press if you wish, freedom of speech is something close to my heart.

I look forward to discussing it with you at the next meeting.

However, I am unaware as to when and where the meeting is, and, if you are serious about liberal democracy you would of course be prepared to engage in face to face talks on the issues you raise. In order to do so I would be happy to turn up at the next Cumbernauld branch meeting if you are prepared to tell me when and where it is to be held.

hugh

Don't Vote for an Idiot, Vote for a Clown

From: hannayrosemary@hotmail.com
To: hughodonnell@cix.co.uk
Subject: Jamie Stone the next Lib Dem Leader
Date: Wed, 19 Sep 2001 14:21

Hello again Hughie,

When you stood in Falkirk West I remember you saying that SNP policies were like nailing jelly to the wall and holding up a blank piece of paper. Hugh, did you know that everyone at the hustings, including Lib Dems, thought you were a plonker? I would sooner have voted for the big daft Socialist bloke (who later went berserk and was charged by the police and had to stand down at the General election) than a wee, bald, effete part time assistant to Gaga Gorrie.

Liz Quigley from the BBC, who is now lumbered with swizzle stick Sweeney, turned to me and bawled, 'Who is that stupid lookin' eejit?' I replied, 'You should have seen the rest!'

And that's the problem and why we need visionary people like Jamie Stone to lead us. A man unafraid to eyeball Mike Tyson and denounce him as a blackguard and a ruffian. A man fearless enough to wear a charcoal suit with a wide grey pinstripe and Day-Glo pink tie in the Parliament. A man who in his last e-mail to me acknowledged that Hugh O'Donnell resembles something that Richard Branson could use to traverse the Atlantic!!

Let's face it Hughie, you now know I am a member of the Lib Dems in Cumbernauld but you have no idea who.

Comes the hour comes the man – Jamie Stone MSP!!!

Lovely chatting with you Hughie

Dr. Rose Hannay

From: hughodonnell@cix.co.uk
To: hannayrosemary@hotmail.com
Subject: RE: Jamie Stone the next Lib Dem Leader
Date: Thurs, 20 Sep 2001 15:28

This is no longer funny or remotely intellectually entertaining. It is simply childish. I would have thought someone doing a postgraduate course had better things to do with their time. I certainly do.

You are no lib dem from cumbernauld or anywhere else.

Goodbye

From: hannayrosemary@hotmail.com
To: jamie.stone.msp@scottish.parliament.uk
Subject: Leadership Challenge
Date: Thurs, 20 Sep 2001 11:06

Hi Jamie,

I think you must have a snitch in your office. I have had 2 sinister e-mails from that desiccated old woman Hugh O'Donnell and he knows about our proposal to nominate you as party leader! He pretended to be a stranger and denied he was a Lib Dem!?! He has clearly lost ownership of his marbles.

You may have come across Hughie. He stood here at the General Election and in Falkirk West in the by-election after Canavan's pantomime. He looks like a cross between a Pox Doctor's Assistant and a constipated chimp. Hugh epitomises everything that is wrong in the party, verbal diarrhoea, banal ideas and a face like a fish supper.

I think Jim Wallace is using him as an agent provocateur. This means they are rattled!! Jamie, watch your (exquisitely coutured) back.

Drop me a line if you can make head or tails of this Byzantine factionalism.

Best Regards
Dr. Rosemary Hannay

Don't Vote for an Idiot, Vote for a Clown

From: Rosemary Hannay:hannayrosemary@hotmail.com
Sent: 24 September 2001 22:05
To: nicola.sturgeon.msp@scottish.parliament.uk
Subject: Leadership

Hello Nicola,
I caught you being interviewed by that wee toad Brian Taylor outside the conference with Lloyd and Fiona Hyslop. I was very impressed by your authority and, dare I say it, gravitas. I am always astonished at such gifts in one so young. (Well, at least compared to me.) I have no doubt that you will be the next leader of the SNP and the first woman 'First Minister' of the modern parliamentary period.

Could I offer a little advice as an 'elder' party member? You need to smile more. You have a beautiful wee face but you tend to impart an aura of intense concentration leading to the perception that you are a little morose, not to say miserable. Also it was striking the splash of colour provided by Fiona's cerise jacket and Lloyd's sunburst yellow hair. (I have heard that a number of the MSPs are openly gay! His hair looks as if it has 'come out' on its own.)

I only ever see you wear dreary grey suits. That only contributes to the patina of melancholia and despondency. You will have seen the stories about Wendy Alexander having a 'make over' during the holidays. She looks almost human now! Something in pastel would be nice on you. Avoid anything that Dorothy-Grace would countenance.

I have just reread this letter and fear I may have over stepped the line and caused offence (and appeared somewhat eccentric.) Please drop me a line to say you have taken my comments in the comradely spirit they are offered?

Dr. Rosemary Hannay

From: Nicola.Sturgeon.msp@scottish.parliament.uk
To: 'Rosemary Hannay' hannayrosemary@hotmail.com
Subject: RE: Leadership
Date: Tues, 25 Sep 2001 09:53:06 +0100

Dear Rosemary
Thank you for your message. Please be assured that I have taken no offence – I appreciate your advice and will take it on board.
Best wishes, Nicola

Nicola and the makeover

From: Rosemary Hannay [mailto:hannayrosemary@hotmail.com]
Sent: 28 September 2001 11:15
To: nicola.sturgeon.msp@scottish.parliament.uk
Subject: makeover

Hi Nicola,

I watched you on TV yesterday and was ecstatic to see that you have taken my advice and given yourself a makeover. The smudge of lip gloss and the splash of warpaint worked brilliantly on the box.

I noted also that you were grinning away like an eejit!! Well done. A little thought to your attire and we will have imperceptibly transformed you from a wee, nippy, irascible, ugly-duckling into a beautiful, sophisticated, political swan.

On the question of clothes can I suggest you seek the advice of Margo Macdonald? Obviously, only a moron would ask Margo for political advice but on coiffure and couture our 'blonde bombshell' has been around the block a few times. (Contrast this with poor old Dorothy-Grace! Some people are just unfathomable on fashion.) Don't let the fact that the clothes look hellish on Margo blind you to her infinite good taste and elegance.

The main thing is that you shone and literally leaped out of the screen making the rest of the scruffy, stuffed shirts on our benches look like dreary, superannuated, civil servants.

Nicola, would you like me to send you weekly reports on how you are coming across on TV? It will be no bother but I don't want to intrude if you'd rather I didn't. A simple Yea or Nea will suffice. Looking forward to hearing from the next leader of the SNP!!

Dr. Rosemary Hannay

PS. On consideration perhaps you should ease up on the facepaint though, there is a fine line between aesthetic discrimination and vulgarity!

From: Nicola.Sturgeon.msp@scottish.parliament.uk
To: Hannayrosemary@hotmail.com
Subject: RE: makeover
Date: Fri, 28 Sep 2001 20:22

Weekly reports would be great and I await them with trepidation!!
Thanks, Nicola

From: Rosemary Hannay
To: Nicola Sturgeon MSP
Subject: Screen Presence
Sent: 04 Oct 2001 10:41

Hi Nicola,

As promised, here is my weekly report on your media profile. Two
sightings this week, once at the Education Ctte. And once today
asking 'Thicko' McLeish a probing question on tobacco advertising.

Unfortunately, on both occasions you were wearing a hideous wee
broon suit. That aesthetic crime was compounded by an equally
dowdy, plain, broon jumper. Jings!!

I know I suggested you ease up on the face paint but to abandon it
totally as you have done is a mega mistake. On TV you have the
pallor of a peely wally vampire!! Talk about the Bride of Dracula!!
Crivens!!

You must urgently do something about that 'bunnet' masquerading
as a hair-do. Do you really aspire to look like a nightmarish
amalgam of Ann Widecombe and a grumpy bearded collie? Help
ma' boab!!

So points out of ten this week? 0/10. Dazzling smiles to camera?
Zero!

Contrast this with the photo of dopey Wendy in today's Herald.
Three types of jewellery, beautifully cut ivory jacket, radiant auburn
hair and lipsticked mouth pouting in a coquettish giggle. OK, her
politics are crapulous but not her costume!

Nicola, I am trying to be constructive but if you'd rather I kept my
opinions to myself just say so. Next week I intend to be brutally
frank if you haven't pulled your socks up.

Rosemary

From: Rosemary Hannay [mailto:hannayrosemary@hotmail.com]
Sent: 21 October 2001 23:18
To: nicola.sturgeon.msp@scottish.parliament.uk
Subject: Weekly Screen Presence Review

Hi Nicola,

Here's my weekly update on your media profile. Only one sighting this week at the Press Conference you gave to the reptiles of the Scottish press.

Unfortunately, no improvement in your screen presence! You were wearing a grey jacket obviously sourced from 'What Every Woman Wants' (if not 'Paddy's Market') and a top that resembled an old fashioned football strip, purple (!?!) with a white, T-shirt collar. Nicola, I've seen better dressed vagrants selling the Big Issue.

The 'slap' you were wearing came out a garish orange on TV and appeared to have been misapplied by an inebriated plasterer. The ghastly mane is still a pure sight! It reminds one of a petulant marmoset sporting a mangy busby.

You are in desperate need of drastic cosmetic and couturial repackaging. Fortunately, I will be in Edinburgh next Friday and have persuaded my coiffeuse, Dionne, to accompany me to advise on reconstructive surgery to your napper. I will also have Amelia, my granddaughter who works at M&S and can give pointers on dress sense. (Of which, you seem to be utterly bereft!!)

We'll pop through your door at 09:30 unless I hear from you that it is inconvenient. Looking forward to discussing your wardrobe with you in person.

Dr. Rosemary Hannay

(Did you watch Roseanna Cunningham on the Holyrood programme today? Neat hair, a sophisticated chiffon scarf and a jacket which matched. Although the ponderous earrings were tawdry and ludicrous for a Sunday morning.)

From: Nicola Sturgeon MSP
To: Hannayrosemary
Subject: RE: Weekly Screen Presence Review
Date: Mon, 22 Oct 11:58

Rosemary

Thanks as usual for your opinions.

Can I respectfully suggest however that you get the colour on your TV checked – I don't possess either a grey jacket or a purple top with a white collar.

I do appreciate objective comments but given the nature of yours, I fear that I may be beyond help in your eyes. In some respects I think we may just have very different tastes – for example, some of the people that you have held up to me as screen role models are people that I think look ghastly on TV.

I am afraid I won't be in Edinburgh on Friday so we will have to meet some other time (although before I agree to take advice from your hairdresser, perhaps I should ask to see a photograph of you!!!)

Best wishes
Nicola

From: HannayRosemary
To: Nicola Sturgeon MSP
Subject: Media profile
Sent: Thurs, 01 Nov 2001 08:32

Hello Nicola,

I caught you on Newsnight with that glaikit article Tom McCabe MSP and the obese and absurd Alex Johnstone MSP.

Let me say immediately that you looked fantastic. The red jacket and black polo neck screamed 'here is a strong, confident woman who doesn't suffer fools gladly and will bite yer heid aff at the neck if you give me any snash.'

The other two looked as if they had been dressed by 'Tramps R Us'.

With the minimum support from 'Fatty Johnstone' you really made McCabe squirm. As usual it's not what he said but what he didn't say which counts. So, It looks like McConnell will be first Minister before Xmas. Is this better or worse for us?

I will say nothing about your haircut as your last letter indicated that you intend to persist with it despite my imprecations. However, at the risk of provoking your ire, can I say a word about smiles towards camera. Last night there were none! Granted a supercilious sneer played about your lips and facial expressions of haughty disdain hinted at condescension. But on TV you have to semaphore your emotions to the audience. A contemptuous grin or a ribald snort lets the public know what you are thinking and can often discombobulate the opposition.

Still, I don't want to nit-pick. 8/10 for appearance!!

Rosemary

PS. If you want me to desist you only have to say so. Otherwise I'll send you a report after First Ministers Questions today.

PPS. I have had the colour checked on my TV, you were right it was wonky. Strangely there was too much colour. Now you look even more peally wally!?!

101 Boghall St
Moodiesburn
Glasgow G69 1DS

20/05/02

John Swinney MSP
The Scottish Parliament

Dear John,

Undoubtedly you saw Dinwoodie's mischievous piece in last Friday's Herald. He ridiculed Thursday's debate as a 'grovelling motion about the contribution of her majesty' on the occasion of her golden jubilee. First he reproduced the quotation from Keir Hardie, viz. 'The toady who crawls through the mire of self-abasement to enable him to bask in the smile of royalty is a victim of a diseased organism.' Second he claimed, 'I am sure that many MSPs, especially from the Labour and SNP benches, are squirming with embarrassment at the sycophantic, servile, forelock-touching motion. . .'

Then the bombshell! 'There were a series of bland but craven speeches, not least from John Swinney of the SNP'. I was so incensed that I consulted the full text of your speech and found it no more abject than that of the other party leaders.

Imagine my astonishment this morning in opening my paper to discover a letter from Gordon John MacKay who styles himself, 'Director of Campaigns', Young Scots for Independence, which said, 'Last Thursday was surely the most shameful day in the short history of our parliament.'

He further said, '. . . it seems [the] chamber is almost entirely populated by kowtowing monarchists' and 'How serious can these cowards be about tackling poverty in Scotland when they line up with the forces of imperialism to bow down before the embodiment of inequality in our society? They have traded their consciences for their 50,000 quid salaries.'

John, how are we ever to move towards independence when people like this will not keep it zipped while you and your colleagues battle against a hostile press, three unionist parties and the 70% of the Scottish public who in poll after poll prove that they are monarchical morons?

Can this young man remain in the party when he targets our MSPs as 'shameful cowards'?

Yours Sincerely
Asinder Khan

Scottish National Party
107 McDonald Road
Edinburgh EH7 4NW

28 th May 2002

Asinder Khan
101 Boghall St
Moodiesbum
GLASGOW G69 1DS

Dear Asinder,

Thank you for your letter of 2 May 2002. I am glad you took the trouble to actually read the speech that I delivered in Parliament. I certainly wouldn't be happy to have it described as bland although I would take great exception to have been described as craven. Journalists are entitled to their opinions but it is more than a little frustrating when some of our own Party colleagues indulge the press with the type of comments that have quite clearly irritated you.

On many of these issues I take the view that you have got to have broad shoulders to be involved in politics and be able to take criticism when it is made. It doesn't make it any less frustrating but it is one of the harsh realities of political life.

I am grateful you took the trouble to write to me with your views.
JOHN SWINNEY MSP, National Convener

Don't Vote for an Idiot, Vote for a Clown

From: Rosemary Hannay
To: John Swinney MSP
Subject: Dorothy-Grace Elder MSP
Sent: Tues, 9 Oct 2001

Hello John,

I have just learned (from the Sunday Times) that you had to unceremoniously eject Dorothy-Grace Elder from your office and that you were provoked into employing an 'expletive'. Well Done!!

It's about time someone had the bottle to tell D-G to F. . . Off (Your favoured unparliamentary term, I believe.) She continually brings the party into disrepute by her wildly, aberrant behaviour (i.e. unarmed combat with Police cuddies outside Govanhill Swimming Pool), rambling, incoherent, abrasive interventions in the chamber and criminal dress sense.

The last time I was canvassing with her in Easterhouse she was wearing that Day-Glo yellow raincoat, wee royal blue bootees and was clutching a postbox red handbag!! This is Easterhoose mind! People were dodging between buses crossing the street to body-swerve her.

John, the ST reported the confrontation concerned the 5000 quid for central resources. Is it really just a question of 'deep pockets and short erms' or are we talking 'psychological flaws'?

Between you and I, the rumour here in Baillieston is that D-G is manoeuvring to be expelled so she can join her friends in the SWP. The word is McAllion is at the same game with New Labour!

John, can I count on your discretion on this information? Could you drop me a line saying nothing I have said will reach a certain glaikit article?

Regards

Dr. Rosemary Hannay

PS. I shook your hand at the Perth Conference, a few years ago, we were laughing about the reintroduction of beaver to Scotland. I don't suppose you remember, you meet so many old Trouts like me!

NO REPLY

From: Rosemary Hannay hannayrosemary@hotmail.com
Sent: 14 October 2001 16:49
To: murray.tosh.msp@scottish.parliament.uk
Subject: TV Appearance

Hi Murray,

Your colleague Kenneth Gibson has agreed to take part in a TV advertising campaign I am organising for the Meat Marketing Board (MMB). The Campaign will roll out in the spring of 2002 and will afford a great deal of exposure to the participating parliamentarians.

In the interests of reciprocity we are seeking one MSP from each of the other parties. Kenny suggested that you have a sense of the absurd and might be interested in taking part.

The advert will be as follows: – Clip of the First Minister droning on at FMQs.

Cut to MSP who bursts out 'The First Minister is talking Mince'.

Cut to FM looking askance and back to MSP who with a rapturous demeanour declares 'Scottish Mince'.

Followed by the logo of the MMB and voiceover extolling the gustatory merits of Scottish meat products.

The £500 appearance fee can be paid to your party or to a youth or community group in your constituency. I will write to you formally with details but could you e-mail me to say if you would be interested in considering such a project?

Looking forward to hearing from you

Dr. Rosemary Hannay

From: Murray.Tosh.msp@scottish.parliament.uk
To: Rosemary Hannay
Subject: RE: TV Appearance
Sent: Thurs, 1 Nov 2001

Sorry, I overlooked this.

I've thought about it carefully, and I don't really feel that it is me.

Murray Tosh

Don't Vote for an Idiot, Vote for a Clown

From: Archie Beatty [mailto:snash@maxies.fsnet.co.uk]
Sent: 09 May 2001 16:30
To: jim.wallace.msp@scottish.parliament.uk
Subject: Criminal justice

Hi Jim,

I am a Lib Dem supporter from Cumbernauld. Have you seen today's Scotsman? That ignorant article Alison Hardie wrote, 'the Lib Dems. . . empty vessels who traded manifesto commitments for ministerial Mondeos.' She really is a poisonous dwarf.

I will be in Edinburgh next Tuesday and intend to go into the Scotsman offices (I used to work there and still have my pass) and whisker her one on the snout. I will then come up to your office to await the police. If all goes according to plan I will be there around 10.30.

One question, will you be able to swing something as my case goes through the criminal justice system?

Regards
Archie Beatty

From: Easton A (Alistair) on behalf of Wallace J (Jim) MSP
To: Archie Beatty
Sent: Fri, 11/05/01 11:31
Subject: Criminal Justice

Dear Mr Beatty,

Jim Wallace has asked me to thank you for your message. While he shares your views on the article in the Scotsman, he cannot of course condone violence!

Regards,

Alistair Easton,
Parliamentary Assistant

From: Archie Beatty
To: Alistair.Easton@scottish.parliament.co.uk
Sent: Sat, 12/05/01 10:07
Subject: Criminal Justice

Hi Alastair,
I was thrilled to get an e-mail from the Minister of Justice (or Goofy as he is affectionately known in our house). I take on board what you said about Jim being unable to publicly condone violence against journalists. But I did note that he didn't advise me not to do it. I think we both know what that means!

So come Tuesday Ms. Hardie is going to be on the receiving end of a boot up the backside and I intend to shout 'THIS IS FROM JIM WALLACE' so all her colleagues in the newsroom are left in no doubt that you don't mess with Jim.

As agreed I'll then come up to your office to await being 'lifted'. Do you think we should call a Press Conference for the arrest?
See you Tuesday

Archie

From: Archie Beatty [mailto:snash@maxies.fsnet.co.uk]
Sent: 15 May 2001 16:30
To: jim.wallace.msp@scottish.parliament.uk
Subject: Criminal justice

Dear Jim,
Sorry I couldn't get in to see you before the election as I was indisposed. Yesterday I had a visit, at my home, from two Detective Constables from Lothian and Border Police. It seems you have a snitch in your office.

I was astonished to learn from DC Marshall that they were from the Parliament's Political Police Unit!! (DC Gibson was a sinister, taciturn and frankly ugly character). Is this outfit's existence public knowledge? Can we as Lib Dems support an unaccountable secret police force? The officers bluntly warned me not to go within two miles of 'The Scotsman'. They left me nursing a violently bleeding nose with blood and snotters all over the walls and carpets.

As a result I obviously vehemently support you in your efforts to have complaints against the police investigated independently!! But not by lawyers!!! Lawyers, as you know only too well, are a bigger bunch of crooks than the Police.

Yours,

Archie Beatty

PS. They haven't banned me from the Parliament so I'll try to pop in to see you before the recess so we can discuss gratuitous police behaviour. Say hello to DC Marshall if you see him. (Although, for your own wellbeing, I strongly advise you not to comment on his impenetrable Edinburgh accent.)

Ben Wallace and the Portillistas

From: Rosemary Hannay [hannayrosemary@hotmail.com
Sent: 10 August 2001 12:05
To: ben.wallace.msp@scottish.parliament.uk
Subject: ballot

Dear Ben,

I know you were a Portillo man, fair enough. Each to their own. Not my cup of tea I'm afraid. Although homophobia is very far from being a factor in my attitude. No, I just don't like Italians. Period.

Like you my husband was a military man for most of his life. So I would appreciate your views on who you think should be supported in the membership ballot.

Our Chairman, Mrs McBride, informs me that the ballot papers will be out in the next week or so.

I see Archie and Francis have announced a plague on both their houses but since we have to choose one, that is a little unhelpful. Although I agree that IDS is a ditch-dull nonentity and a recipe for four more years of internecine strife and Kenneth is an obese, sybarite who will split the Conservative party in two.

Dear Ben help!!

Dr. Rosemary Hannay

From: Ben.Wallace.msp@scottish.parliament
To: Rosemary Hannay
Subject: RE: Ballot
Sent: Mon, 13 Aug 2001

Dear Dr Hannay,

I would be most grateful if you could e-mail me your address and tel. number.

Thank you

Ben

Don't Vote for an Idiot, Vote for a Clown

From: Rosemary Hannay hannayrosemary@hotmail.com
Sent: Tues, 14 Aug 2001
To: ben.wallace.msp@scottish.parliament.uk
Subject: Tory Ballot

Ben,

What on earth is the matter with you flippin' Portillistas?
Can't you ever stop the sinister Machiavellian machinations? I simply requested a little advice from an ex-officer and, I thought, a gentleman. I don't want to be signed up for your faction! I won't be supplying information from my association! And I won't be helping your faction to 'influence' the outcome of the ballot!

This continual faction fighting, back stabbing and absence of integrity has for too long characterised our party. Is it any wonder the public view us as the party of Jeffrey Archers, Neil and Christine Hamiltons and Jonathan Aitkens? Fantasists, jailbirds and crooks. Your pathetic malevolent response to my request for advice has pushed me over the edge and I am now seriously considering if I wish to remain in an organisation made up of blinkered ideological pygmies.

Indignantly
Dr. Rose Hannay

From: Ben Wallace MSP
To: Rosemary Hannay
Subject: RE: Tory Ballot
Sent: Tues, 14 Aug 2001

Look, I only asked for your details as verification of your identity. I get daily e-mails from UFO spotters to devious journalists. You may be aware that anybody can set up a hotmail account on e-mail without any checks!
I do not deserve such a vitriolic reply. This has nothing to do with ideology or Machiavelli, I merely want to speak to you directly.
I do not know what gives you the right to talk to me like dirt but I have a responsibility to the Party and members to satisfy my office of the security surrounding a request. As an ex-military man, who was target by the IRA and who has since been threatened while in Parliament I have to protect my security, so I would appreciate a little understanding.

From: Rosemary Hannay: hannayrosemary@hotmail.com
Sent: 14 August 2001 17:05
To: ben.wallace.msp@scottish.parliament.uk
Subject: Apology

Ben,

I have obviously disastrously misjudged the situation and am distraught to have caused such gratuitous offence. I am a 'bear of very little brain'. I totally accept that the splenetic tone I adopted was unforgivable. Especially to another conservative.

I thought you were only after my vote!! I hope you can find it in your heart to forgive a silly old fool who should really be horse whipped for her impetuosity. (What's our line on corporal punishment?)

I can quite see how the bad guys could target you through your computer and that dispensing advice willy nilly would compromise your security.

I've decided to vote for Iain Duncan Smith. He is a plain man and no Einstein but I think we Tories need a little pedestrian leadership after the rollercoaster we got from William.

I am sorry you became so incensed at my cretinism. I know when I have a tantrum, deep breaths often help. I will not bother you again but do I have your permission to show our correspondence to Mrs McBride and other members of my association?

Rose

From: ben.wallace.msp@scottish.parliament.uk
To: Rosemary Hannay
Subject: RE: Apology
Sent: Wed, 15 Aug 2001

Dear Rose,

I would be most grateful if you could just let me know your association and your address before I can authorise the passing of my correspondence.

I did ask in the last e-mail and I am happy to talk to you.

Ben

Don't Vote for an Idiot, Vote for a Clown

From: Rosemary Hannay: hannayrosemary@hotmail.com
Sent: 15 August 2001
To: Ben.Wallace.msp@scottish.parliament.uk
Subject: Visit to parliament

Dear Ben,

Great news! In your last missive you said 'I am happy to talk to you.'

Well next Wednesday you will and in person.

Mrs McBride our chairman has to be in Edinburgh professionally and she has agreed to let me accompany her! [Unfortunately, I had already shown her your e-mails. At first she threatened to box your ears but I persuaded her that I was culpable. Frankly, she is a bit of a scarey Dragon.]

So unless I hear from you that it is inconvenient, Angela and I will come up to your office at the parliament and pop through your door at 09:30 hrs precisely.

Regards
Rose

From: ben.wallace.msp@scottish.parliament.uk
To: Rosemary Hannay
Subject: RE: Visit to parliament
Sent: Thurs, 16 Aug 2001

Great news, but unfortunately I am away from Friday with my fiancée in Wales (my summer holiday). So I will not be able to meet. I am however extremely interested to meet you and Mrs McBride. (But please let me know your association and branch.) And can happily meet in September.

Ben

Ben Wallace and the Portillistas

From: Rosemary Hannay:hannayrosemary@hotmail.com
Sent: 07 September 2001 11:57
To: ben.wallace.msp@scottish.parliament.uk
Subject: Visit

Hello again Ben,

Angela McBride and I will be in Edinburgh next Thursday.

Will it be OK for us to drop in to your office for a cup of tea, a bun and a bit of a chinwag? Is there wheelchair access and are well-behaved dogs allowed on the premises? We'll bring the buns!!

So unless we hear to the contrary we'll surge through your door next Thursday about 09:30.

Dr. Rosemary Hannay (Angela and Max the dog, he will have his muzzle on)

From: ben.wallace@scottish.parliament.uk
To: Rosemary Hannay
Subject: RE: Visit
Sent: Tues, 11 Sep 2001

Dear Rosemary,

Good to hear from you. I would be most grateful if you could let me know which date you intend for you visit and I am sorry to push but also your branch and association?

Ben Wallace

From: Archie Beatty
Sent: 10 May 2001 11:53
To: mike.watson.msp@scottish.parliament.uk
Subject: Year Zero

Hi Mike,
I have just finished reading your interesting and informative book 'Year Zero'. I thoroughly enjoyed it. I intend to make sure our library gets any future works you publish.

One question if I may. On page 96 you deal with the Rafferty affair and you say 'He (Mr Rafferty) was unable to disown allegations that he had wrongly briefed journalists that Health Minister Susan Deacon had received death threats. . . '

I have showed this sentence to Mrs Beatty and to John our next door neighbour, who is a staunch Labour man, and none of us can make head nor tails of it. Did he brief reporters or not? That's my question. Looking forward to hearing from you.
Yours Sincerely
Archie Beatty

PS. This is the first e-mail my wife and I have sent (I'm 75) our grandson Robert has helped us!

From: Mike.Watson.msp@scottish.parliament.uk
Sent: Thurs, 10/05/01 13:01
To: Archie Beatty
Subject: RE: Year Zero

Dear Archie,
Many thanks for your message and for your kind words about my book; I'm very glad you enjoyed it. My purpose in writing Year Zero was simply to record some impressions of the Parliament's first year from the inside and I did not want it to be written solely from a Labour Party viewpoint – hence my decision to interview MSPs from all of the major parties.

It has been quite well received by my colleagues, who are usually the harshest judges! I have no intention of writing another one, at least until I retire from the Parliament; it was extremely time-consuming and the job of an MSP is pretty demanding anyway. My partner Clare was very understanding about the fact that I had to spend every spare minute in the period July-September 2000 writing the book – even to the extent that I took my laptop with me to Tunisia for our holiday! But I felt it was worth doing as a project and the reaction of people such as yourself make it seem well worthwhile.

As to the point about the John Rafferty issue. If you recall, it was claimed by journalists that he had let it be known (unofficially, as he was not Donald Dewar's press spokesperson) to journalists that Susan Deacon had received a death threat following an announcement which she had made about an increase in the provision of birth control clinics. The point I was trying to make was that Rafferty was unable to shake off this allegation that he had indeed briefed journalists in this way. My own view is that this was probably for the very good reason that he did indeed do so – although of course Rafferty never admitted it. However, the fact that he resigned his post within 48 hours carries a fairly clear message.
With best wishes
Mike Watson MSP

From: Archie Beatty
Sent: 10 May 2001 17:28
To: mike.watson.msp@scottish.parliament.uk
Subject: Year Zero

Hi Mike,
Many thanks for your amazingly prompt reply. I've never corresponded with a peer before!
I know you must be very busy but could we pose one more question on the book? On page 98 you say 'Seven weeks after Rafferty's departure, Philip Chalmers resigned as head of strategic communications amid circumstances which were never convincingly explained.'

John next door, who has a Labour party membership, says it was in the Daily Record that Mr Chalmers was found drunk in charge of a motor vehicle with an underage sex worker in Blythswood Square. John claims it was not the first time.

If I remember right that bampot Martin Clarke was editor then and he was very hostile to the party. When you say it was never convincingly explained do you mean you don't believe what was in the papers at the time?

Yours Etc. Archie Beatty

From: Mike.Watson.msp@scottish.parliament.uk
Sent: Thurs, 10/05/01 18:29
To: Archie Beatty
Subject: RE: Year Zero
Dear Archie,
In fact, I mean the opposite, i.e. I did believe that what was in the papers was substantially true, though it was never stated officially at the time of his resignation why he had actually gone.
As I said in the book, I was not the only Labour MSP who felt Chalmers had let down the Executive and the Labour group – certainly, his departure was not lamented by us !
Best wishes, Mike Watson MSP
PS Your description of Mr Clarke is kinder than mine would be!

From: Archie Beatty
Sent: Fri. 11/05/01 09:52
To: mike.watson.msp@scottish.parliament.uk
Subject: RE: Year Zero
Hello Mike,
I don't want to be a pest but my wife and I, big John from next door and Sadie from the flats were looking at your e-mails tonight and there's a couple of things we don't get. Wouldn't it have been better just to say 'In my opinion John Rafferty was stone mad and went completely doolally and briefed the press that Susan had received death threats.' We think that would have avoided torturing the English language with phrases like 'he was unable to disown the allegations'. That just looks like you're trying to avoid the bleedin' obvious!

On Philip Chalmers wouldn't it have been better just to say 'he was caught in the red light district with a heroin addict and prostitute and he was mad with the drink and it wasn't the first time and the papers were full of it and Mr Dewar looked like an eejit'? That at least would have had the merit of clarity instead of 'it was never convincingly explained'.

Big John was in Waterstone's the other day and asked how many copies of the book had been sold – 12. We think that's because it was a bit tedious. In fact, it is the most boring, insipid, leaden, mind-numbingly dull tract it has ever been my misfortune to clap eyes on in my 75 years!!

All the best, Archie et al.

From: Rosemary Hannay hannayrosemary@hotmail.com
Sent: 08 August 2001 15:51
To: andrew.wilson.msp@scottish.parliament.uk
Subject: Roads

Andrew,
As someone whose husband worked on the roads for nearly 30 years it comes as no surprise to me that Bear and Amey are making an arse of it. I see from the Herald that you said 'these contracts have been controversial since day one and now they are proving to be extremely troublesome'.

For Christ sake man is that the best the SNP can do – 'proving troublesome'!!!

I know you are constrained by all kinds of pressure in the Party and won't want to get too far from John Swinney's middle of the road (no pun intended, honest) position but I feel we need something a little more vigorous than 'terribly troubling'.

Or am I supposed to tell my friends still on the roads that our position in the SNP is that it is all 'terribly troubling'. Come on Andrew what am I to tell the 'bears' who work on the roads?

Dr. Rose Hannay

From: andrew.wilson.msp@scottish.parliament.uk
To: Rosemary Hannay
Subject: RE: Roads
Sent: Thurs, 9 Aug 2001

Point taken Rosemary.
I am in Dublin just now on holiday and was called without any information on the situation at all. Given that I don't like to fire off until I know the detail.

I know what you mean though and please be assured that I never miss them when I feel they deserve it and I of course in this case believe they do. Just very difficult to be able to do more when I am on my week's annual holiday

Sorry about that for now but watch this space. Would you like to help in pointing me in the right direction with this issue?

Thanks for being in touch and hope to hear back.
Andrew

Don't Vote for an Idiot, Vote for a Clown

From: Gordon.Mulholland@scottish.parliament.uk
To: Rosemary Hannay
Subject: Andrew Wilson e-mail
Sent: Wed, 8 Aug 2001

Dear Dr. Hanney,
Thank you for e-mailing Andrew earlier on today.

Unfortunately he is not in the office today, but I will bring your comments to his attention on his return. For your information I have attached the press quote in its entirety and hope this gives you a fuller picture of Andrew's comments.

Regards
Gordon Mulholland Parliamentary Assistant

From: Rosemary Hannay
To: Gordon Mulholland@scottish.parliament.uk
Subject: Roads
Sent: Thurs, 9 Aug 2001 16:21

Hi Gordon,

Thanks for your prompt reply. I have now had an e-mail from Andrew appointing me to the position of special adviser on roads. Could you please resend me the full quote you referred to as it didn't arrive.

Dr. Rose Hannay

From: Rosemary Hannay
To: Gordon Mulholland@scottish.parliament.uk
Subject: Roads
Sent: Thurs, 16 Aug 2001

Gordon,

I still haven't received the full quote on Roads which Andrew gave to the Herald. Could you expedite its dispatch so that I can get started 'pointing' Andrew in the right direction.

Can't wait to hear from you!

Rosemary Hannay

From: Rosemary Hannay hannayrosemary@hotmail.com
Sent: 20 August 2001 09:10
To: andrew.wilson.msp@scottish.parliament.uk
Subject: Highways

Andrew,
Two things:–
1. I have repeatedly requested Gordon Mulholland to furnish the complete quote you gave to the Herald on Highways, nothing has been forthcoming! Has the indolent rascal gone on holiday?
2. Bravo on your column in today's Sunday Mail. Your 'If Thomas Edison was a Nat, Labour would describe the lightbulb as an anti-candle project' raised a guffaw.

However, in a piece of typical political legerdemain you discussed 'Lord' Mike's call for use of the Tartan Tax for 500 words without saying where we stand on the tax varying powers. Well done. No point divulging our position to the New Labour's poisonous rabble!!

Entre nous, though, are we still in favour of the 'Penny for Scotland' or has it been cast, along with poor Alex Salmond into the deepest pit of hell?
Regards
Dr. Rose Hannay

From: andrew.wilson.msp@scottish.parliament.uk
To: Rosemary Hannay
Subject: RE: Highways
Sent: Tues, 21 Aug 2001

Thanks.
Gordon will be in touch, I understand he has already sent you stuff? The line was very quickly quoted down the phone from Dublin.

Anyway, on the other matter, we have to say 'we will announce in due course' no more or less. Our tax stance is as outlined in the election manifesto and we will revisit in a Scottish Parliamemt context when it suits. Sorry there is not more to it just now, but that in my view and experience is the most appropriate position for us to take.

Best regards Andrew
PS Cut to the quick with the 'best looking MSP' statement sent to Dunc, you should see him up close. It's all make-up!!!

From: Archie Beatty
To: andrew.wilson.msp@scottish.parliament.uk
Subject: Beef
Sent: Mon, 21 May 2001

Hi Andrew,

I am a 75-year-old SNP member from Moodiesburn. My wife and I met you at the Tesco at Craigmarloch one Saturday and we were very impressed. We are 110% behind your brave stance on litter. Moodiesburn is one big tip and our collie dug Max has cut his paws on broken glass 5 times in the last year. (It's no surprise vets are the wealthiest people around – 65 quid fur a coupla stitches in a paw!?!)

I hope you won't be offended if I raise a personal point with you. Two weeks ago I was sitting having a cup of tea watching the Sunday edition of the Holyrood programme. When my wife came through with a few scones, she looked at the screen and said 'Is that the boy we met at the supermarket? Christ!! . . . he's fair put on the beef!!

I noticed that one of the prizes you offered in today's Sunday Mail for the litter slogan was 'Motherwell's first game next season with pies and pint'. This may be the problem, eh?

You don't want to stand up in the chamber, about to destroy the Blairites economic policy to be met with a chorus of 'Who ate all the pies, who ate all the pies, you fat B_____d etc.'

You're a good man with figures but you must do something about yours. Nobody likes a fat monetarist! Remember Nigel Lawson.

You are the youngest MSP in Parliament (26 I believe), you have a great future infront of you but not if you look like a Scottish Zeppelin. I hope you are not offended by my forthright comments and accept them in the comradely spirit in which they are offered.

Do you still have your surgery at Tesco's? I'd like to meet you again.

Yours Sincerely
Archie Beatty